Service Dog Project

The Creative Training of Great Danes and the Impressive Service Dogs They Become

Directed by & content from
Carlene White

Compiled & narrated by
Janice Anne Wheeler

©2020

The fine print.

We used real names unless folks asked us not to. Most people and animals associated with our organization are thrilled to be part of it and want to give it as much exposure as possible. The Service Dog Project (SDP) has supporters world-wide who donate generously, watch the cameras frequently and offer both advice and hands-on assistance when they are called upon unless it's geographically impossible. It's a diverse, interesting, warm-hearted group of very dedicated employees and volunteers. Many of those involved observe that, when you show up, you are treated as family. It feels like a family. And they are right.

The Doggie Daily email excerpts included here have not been edited for spelling, grammar or punctuation. These emails are written by Carlene White every morning from SDP headquarters (her desk). Many of the stories and quotes found here were compiled by Janice Anne Wheeler from those daily communications. Some opinions are included to emphasize a point, not to offend or hurt anyone's feelings unnecessarily. We firmly believe in the First Amendment.

The stories from SDP partners, volunteers, recipients and/or their families, received via email, have not been edited for content, grammar or punctuation.

You will find commentary from Janice Anne Wheeler in the first person which was derived from interviews, conversations, research and personal observations. These recollections are as accurate as the human memory allows and her opinions are not intended as fact.

Cover Photo:
Carlene White with future Great Dane Service Dogs
Boo, Mischief, Hank, Tony, Goldie, George, Lars, Blue, Sienna and Ariot

Back Cover: Bella Burton with adult Service Dog George

to tiffany and deagle
the roots of it all

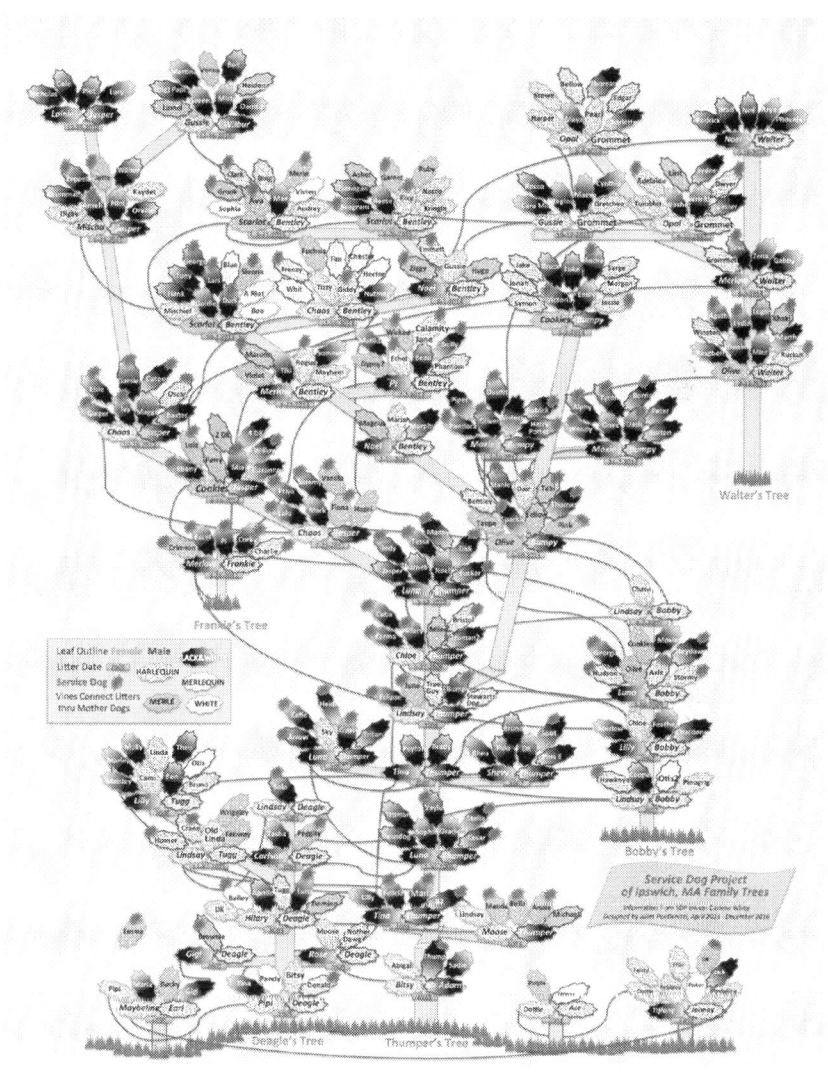

Table of Contents

MY INTRODUCTION

I saw her melt. I didn't think it was possible but I saw her melt. It was a moment in time when she and I were posing for a picture, just the two of us. And then we added a puppy. One of her puppies. And she melted. It's that simple. A transformation occurred when she saw that beautiful Great Dane, when she touched it and held it and talked to it. She melted. She is tough on the outside, soft in the middle. No bulls**t all around. I think that was why I was so drawn to her, why I wanted to write this book, tell her story, emphasize how incredibly she has impacted so many lives.

I am describing Carlene White, the rather intimidating leader and creator of the Service Dog Project. She does nothing if it's not above and beyond. She is fascinated with logistics, she tells it like it is, and she makes things happen. From what I understand, her entire life has been spent making unusual, (sometimes unilateral, sometimes unpopular) decisions. She built, from the ground up, this incredibly caring, energetic, creative non-profit in Ipswich, Massachusetts. She has set the standard for Mobility Impaired service dogs; the SDP very carefully breeds and raises Great Danes with traits specifically chosen for that purpose: big, strong, intelligent, even-tempered. "Her brain is constantly in motion," one of the many dedicated volunteers told me. "It never shuts off. She is very intelligent, very caring and not cuddly. I love spending time with her." Later during that same interview, she looked straight into my eyes for emphasis. "Carlene invited you here, which means she has an idea that probably none of us have ever heard of. Carlene trumps everything, she's the most important thing."

The Service Dog Project (SDP) has donated over two hundred Great Dane Service Dogs to people with balance issues due to neurological diseases, injuries or any number of other qualifying circumstances. These impressive dogs allow them to achieve greater independence. Veterans, First Responders and their families are given priority. These Danes raise their partner's capabilities and self-confidence to a new normal by providing a mobility support animal who is also intuitive enough to know when emotional adversity is playing a part. That may be the best part of these Great Danes. Their intuition.

SDP's working service dogs are not pets and have received extensive, specific training that works with their own natural abilities. Their dogs are very well educated and experienced, so once a dog is paired with an applicant the dog continues to adjust to the needs of their partner. Certifying one of these dogs comes with a price tag of twenty-seven thousand dollars. Every cent of that is donated outright or raised through an assortment of programs. Some of their care is done by volunteers. Very importantly, these Great Danes are given, free of charge, to the chosen qualified recipients. The dogs provide a priceless service and enhance the quality of life for their partners immeasurably. Is it sometimes challenging to have a one hundred and fifty-pound dog in your care? Absolutely. But I met not a single person who would trade that adversity for their original one.

Carlene White knows she is changing and saving lives. Her own self-sufficiency is incredibly important to her and she is passionate about giving that same independence and freedom to others. Her organization allows her to do that, over and over again. That is the motivation and the reward, and it shows. "This book is telling her about herself," I confided in a SDP dog recipient; he knows she can be intimidating! "It seems a little dangerous, but she's just so unique and driven. I want people to know all about her, and SDP." "Go," he quickly replied. "I agree with you." I am transcribing that conversation this wintery morning so Carlene knows what my purpose is. My purpose is to tell the world how impressive the Service Dog Project is. How liberating it is that people can be given self-confidence, self-sufficiency, and self worth by learning to work with a well educated Great Dane.

In January of 2020 during 5:00pm Daily Mail Call a check was received from a gentleman who gifted to SDP in his will. His generous donation pays for a magnificently educated Great Dane, and the only contingency was that the dog goes to a Veteran in need. The look on Carlene's face? Priceless. SDP brings out the good in people.

Purina® knows the value of Carlene's work as well. They now donate food from the Pro Plan "Savor" line of products, which she had purchased for over three decades. Now, in a beautifully choreographed performance, the nine pallets of dry and canned food are delivered bi-monthly down the very narrow driveway with a very large truck. Each pallet is unloaded and stored in one minute and twenty-eight seconds! Purina's generosity is valued at nearly seventy thousand dollars a year, and very much appreciated.

You can watch that delivery dance on Explore.org! Kudos to that organization (more on them later in the book) and Dog Bless You for donating the seven live cameras which have enabled a virtual community to develop around the process of whelping, raising and training these priceless service dogs.

Last fall Carlene had attended some community event or other, I have lost track now of which one, the schedule is busy. That group unexpectedly presented her with a sizeable, somewhat surprising check! Carlene promptly tucked that substantial gift into her bra and escaped the public forum. That does not make her any less grateful, she would just rather be melting with her pups and making sure the rest of her dogs are safely at rest in the Massachusetts woods.

YOUR INTRODUCTION TO CARLENE WHITE

This book explores Carlene White's greatest innovation. She singlehandedly created a non-profit, bare-bones organization that makes people's lives better. Service Dog Project Inc. is a registered 501c3 and is fully accredited by Assistance Dogs International. On a more casual level, the farm is affectionately referred to as "Crazy Acres." There are creatures with fur and feathers, hooves and paws. Everything has a purpose, often more than one, and every day everybody gets a little love and at least one lesson.

There are great tales of accomplishment, praise, laughter and insight. There are children who can walk down the halls in school instead of being bound to a wheelchair, walker or crutches. There is a Veteran who tried to take his own life. Now, with the help of his Great Dane service dog, he is able to travel the country spreading his message about suicide prevention and asking for help when you need it. There are many, many more great stories.

The most impactful comments are from the folks with a Great Dane service dog actually at their side. Honestly, I found so many comments impactful that I cannot even begin to include them all here. I included an additional sampling at the end in a chapter entitled *More dog stories you will love*. Some of the most memorable comments are from those who love the people who received the dogs. These are just the tip of the iceberg of who is positively impacted by Carlene's Project.

SDP is located on a very well-utilized twelve-acre property with barns, storage sheds, horse stalls, outdoor kitchen, ponds, a chicken coop, laundry rooms, guest houses for recipients (and anyone else connected), forested runs for the dogs to roam and a large arena for educating. All kennels are heated and air conditioned with in/out doors and second story sleeping lofts. These areas provide the necessary space to raise the dogs from birth until graduation and even back for retirement if needed. All puppies reside at the farm until they are matched or adopted elsewhere. SDP has grown to include over one hundred and forty volunteers and is the home of thirty, often as many as fifty, dogs: some learning, some breeding, all an important part of the operation.

Carlene, at age eighty-two, works on her Project all day every day. When she asked me to write this book she warned me that we needed to get started right away. "I don't even buy the large size toothpaste", she confided in me, somehow knowing I would understand. Life is short. Get going, do what needs to be done! And she goes and goes and goes. She is currently receiving oral chemotherapy treatment for Breast Cancer after surgery last spring. You would never guess. It does not seem to slow her down. "In the summer I have to go to bed in the daylight," she says regretfully. When the summer sun in Massachusetts rises around 4:30 Carlene is already at her computer, coffee in hand.

During my first stay there were thirteen puppies in the same building as her office, her kitchen, her living room and her bedroom. It is her home, a beautiful log structure complete with striking stone fireplace and washable floors. There is absolutely no doggie smell or odor. There is twenty-four-hour staff which often catches the poo before it hits the washable floor. Now, most importantly, it is a place where service dogs are raised specifically to make people's lives better.

The five week old puppies have our undivided attention on this particular day; they are hard to resist and are already being educated, gently guided, to understand how things work. After eighteen months or so, (up to two years) the dogs are donated to recipients, and no payment from the recipient is required. All expenses, and they are extensive, are paid through donations and grants. A small percentage of the animals are not destined to serve, due to gait or some other personality trait, but are still in high demand as working therapy dogs or appropriately labeled 'perfect pets'.

Carlene's own best friend, Bentley, is a truly magnificent example of the breed. He is regal, graceful, patient, watchful, and the sire of award winning service dogs anyone would be proud of. When he stands up in Carlene's SUV he is tall enough to leave the evidence on the roof in the form of course short hair, lots of it. Bentley, born in 2011, is one of the gentle, intuitive creatures who goes to the nursing homes and makes a difference in those people's lives, too. The two of them have stories beyond your imagination. Both stepped onto an elevator not all that long ago and were electrocuted. The complete effects of this black-out for both man and beast are still unknown, but he has been unable to sire a litter since the incident and that weighs heavily on SDP. There was no 'settlement' as the elevator company's Legal Department indicated the following opinion, "At 79 we will out wait you; just go buy another dog." Those poor lawyers must have a terrible relationship with their dogs- they just go get another like a pair of sneakers.

Carlene and Bentley travel together to represent SDP every chance they get and accept donations to appear in advertisements, photo shoots and an assortment of things you and I have probably never thought of. Seven a.m. Rotary meeting? Sure. Donate blood at the local vet? Absolutely. Midnight run to the Boston airport to pick up pups from Germany with just the right traits? You bet. If it needs to be done, she'll do it.

Service Dog Project (SDP) does more than breed and educate the Great Danes; they also train the recipients. This mathematician turned animal trainer has, as you can imagine, an interesting and varied repertoire, starting with a neighborhood circus seven decades ago. Her daughter, Janine Jacques, who has a PHD and a couple of Master's degrees, wrote *Dogs, Donkeys and Circus Performers* in 2013 if you want even more tales about all the different tails running around Crazy Acres. Together they rescue creatures far and wide; Danes, donkeys, horses, guinea hens, goats, a gentle golden brown mule, whoever needs it, really, and bring them back to Massachusetts. "Janine can be counted on to do what's logical," Carlene described her younger daughter with what I think is the highest compliment she could give anyone. 'Common sense is highly underrated' is a popular theme around here. This is the Animal Episodes logo:

White has a level of humility that is refreshing. "The Danes are smart when they are born," she says, looking at me sideways so I understand the importance of this. "Some people try to train them and wreck 'em! We let them learn, with guidance,

14

and then these dogs do things we didn't train them to do, it's amazing." Carlene and her #1 sidekick and trainer Megan guide these puppies from a very young age into a learning mode so they are well on their way to understanding what their job will become. As young as eight weeks these puppies begin to develop their innate abilities to figure things out.

She lists a few of her favorite examples, "Elvis and Fiona on the rocks in the creek, George and Bella, Wendy and Hunter." The dog's name generally comes before the person's name, as that is also how they stand in importance to Carlene. "The dogs have their own way of looking at things. I try to look from the standpoint of the dog." Educating dogs by their 'Point of View' is often more rewarding and successful than more traditional methods.

That is a big difference in philosophy. These Danes want to help and they don't have a specific command to do so. They solve problems on their own, keeping their person safe. When their service vest is in place, they are working, and they know it. In the last few years, the use of Service Dogs for youth with afflictions such as cerebral palsy has increased with amazing results, and demand is on the rise. Requests for dogs (the form is on the SDP website) stream in via snail mail. Those inquiries are one of the many stacks on Carlene's cluttered desk. If it is a potential match, the person or family is contacted and asked to come and volunteer, spend some time, help out around the place, get to know the operation and understand what it is about. Recipients and volunteers alike just keep showing up, doing what needs to be done. I cannot wait to go back.

This is a small, self-sufficient non-profit. They plow their own snow, build their own buildings, operate an animal rescue program, prepare and deliver bowls and bowls of dog food, manage their own meals, pick up a whole lot of poop. Big poop. And when something goes wrong, somebody needs to fix it. And they do.

The day of my arrival I met a volunteer whose son went to school that week without crutches for the first time ever. The service dog and the freshman (Roo and Ben) learned the ropes of high school together. With the help of his new Great Dane he walked up stairs and down hallways. He walked everywhere he needed to go.

With tears in his eyes, this very willing contributor told me what an incredible difference the Project has made in the life of his family. He reveres what is accomplished on this hallowed ground. People's lives are truly made better. In return, he utilized his engineering background to build a swing set (for adults) one adult being Carlene. Just an hour before I heard his story they were hoisting it upright with the aid of trees, ropes, geometry, a tractor and some unsolicited advice. The mathematician (driving her tractor) and the volunteer engineer got it done with many other hands pulling a little weight. It takes a village. Perhaps the village mentality is why my visit was so impactful to me. This group of people has an impressive, universal goal.

I stayed in the main guest cabin and woke up at three o'clock the second morning, amazed by my surroundings, astounded by what this group of people accomplishes. I realized, perhaps even more than they do, the scope of their impact. The wonderfulness of what they do. While there is definitely a sense of purpose, the daily routines, feeding, cleaning, exercise and laundry become the norm to the employees here. It's how they spend their workdays. There are routine words of praise and an occasional grumble, be assured of that, but they are so close to the Project that it may be easy to lose sight of the individual results when their dogs are matched and go off to a new life. An outsider such as myself can see what an amazing transition they create in people's lives. I constantly compliment everything they accomplish and I often get looks of surprise. Carlene's simple vision with complicated logistics is a reality. They create independence. They liberate people. It's huge.

The Veteran protagonist and co-author of my book *Knot Today* would not be doing what he is doing without the SDP. Without them giving him a Service Dog and a chance to live his life, Scott Aubin would be unable to share his message with others. Without the help of Dash, his one hundred and sixty pound Dane, he would not be able to do the outreach and Suicide Prevention Talks that he does. He would not be able to manage his own PTSD and in turn help people with their own struggles, their own journeys. He is living an amazing life with many positive impacts. He is paying it forward.

"She is a <u>force</u>," Scott told me, describing Carlene. That is quite a descriptor, and we both fall into respectful silence at the thought. "I'm glad you got to experience Crazy Acres," he went on. "That is kind of like sacred grounds for me."

The Service Dog Project creates a fantastic chain reaction. Fantastic! And we probably don't even completely appreciate the scope of it! Families united, kids out of wheel chairs, Veterans leading productive, healthy lives. A law student with Cerebral Palsy able to achieve her dreams. A person finally able to go to a baseball game and a concert; able to do things that the rest of us take for granted. Multiple Sclerosis patients able to keep their jobs, maintain a normal life. These people are living examples of resilience, strength and bravery.

It's that simple. The Service Dog Project (SDP) welcomes everyone; those who need a Service Dog and those who need a purpose. Those who think dogs are better than people, and those who know that people are better when they have dogs.

Carlene started out in the entertainment business, and I imagine she was, even then, educating those she worked with. The poster below gives you a sampling of what she did training and working with Animal Episodes. Thankfully, she moved on to Great Dane Service Dogs and now concentrates on making people's lives better.

17

Animal Episodes "Client's Tail"

WATT REGULATORS
SUFFOCK DOWNS RACE TRACK
PERKINS SCHOOL FOR THE BLIND
NORTH SHORE MUSIC THEATER
GOOD MORNING AMERICA
the

for 30 years
NEXT STOP WONDERLAND
PRUDENTIAL INSURANCE
NEW YORK TIMES 7/3/88
BOSTON GLOBE 11/29/92
UNSOLVED MYSTERIES
LADIES HOME JOURNAL
WITCHES OF EASTWICK
WALL STREET JOURNAL
FLOWERS IN THE ATTIC
HOUGHTON MIFFLIN
EVENING MAGAZINE
BYE BYE AMERICA
HARVARD HEALTH
GOODWILL HUNTING
WANT ADVERTISER
MAXWELL HOUSE
BOSTON RECORD
READERS DIGEST

CLIENT's TAIL

as **ANIMAL EPISODES**

we did **TV**
MOVIES
PRINT ADS

NEXT KARATE KID
ROYAL SONESTA
SWEET AND LOW
N.E. TELEPHONE
DUNKIN DONUTS
COACH LEATHER
AMERICAN BUILT   **WITH**
HOUSE SITTERS
AMERICAN GIRL
HONOR BOUND
RALPH LAUREN
FOUR SEASONS
ISUZU TROOPERS
MASS LOTTERY
WONDERLAND
BROOKSTONE
N.H. LOTTERY
LOVE LETTERS
OPPOSITE SEX
WALT DISNEY
BLOWN AWAY
HOME DEPOT
MACK TRUCK
McDONALDS
USA TODAY
MERMAIDS
DOG WATCH
FLEET BANK
POTPOURRI
N.E SERUM
WOOLRICH
EVEREADY
MARSHALLS
POLAROID
COMPUJET
BUFFERIN
PET USA
FILENES
TALBOTS
UNITECH
LL BEAN
SPORTO
NYNEX
CHEVY
HYATT
KEDS
FORD
BOSE
WGBH
TIME
NBC
ABC
CBS
SAX   **now we**   **train**
BBN
JCC
BBC

		crabs	
	frogs	peacocks	
dogs	turtles	donkeys	pigs
cats	fish	geese	snakes
mice	horses	sheep	swans
cows	ducks	roosters	iguana
goats	rats	cockroaches	
hens	deer	oxen	
	emu	and more	

SERVICE   DOGS

18

CAMERA PEOPLE

We have talked about non-profit creativity right? Explore.org donated and installed live cameras, now numbering seven, all around the property. There are three in the main house and the balance are scattered throughout the buildings used by the Danes for training and sleeping as well as in the barns used for rescuing all those other creatures that need rescuing. You can watch these cameras for free. At any given moment, there are a few hundred people doing exactly that. Watching the Service Dog Project live. Those people are called Camera People (CPs). Who thinks of these things?! So awesome. There are only sixty-three places on the planet that have been given the opportunity to open their world to Explore.org. The chosen few.

There is a certain irony that Carlene White had a long career on the other side of the camera, training all sorts of animals (not just dogs) to work in movies, commercials and special events. Animal Episodes, the business was called, based right there in Massachusetts. A crazy way to make a living, she traveled the country creating perfect moments with animals. "Ellen DeGeneres nearly killed me!" she exclaims, describing how she had to hide in a ditch while filming a shot with the esteemed actress. There are stories of pigeons under her shirt, collecting cockroaches from a restaurant, and the donkeys, oh the donkeys. Up and down the elevators in a five-star Hotel during the holidays, complete with antlers in place, eight donkeys waited with daughter Janine for half an hour or so in the bar while Carlene went to get the truck. She can still picture the sturdy miniatures (just thirty-two inches high at the shoulder) walking between taxi cabs, with her chasing them. "Now how many taxi drivers got accused of being drunk thinking they were passed by a donkey in Boston traffic?" she asks me, laughing. "Those donkeys pulled me out of more problems. They have a lot more common sense than people." This is how Carlene chooses her favorite creatures on the planet. Common sense. Regardless, let it be known that Carlene knows a bit about cameras. And now she is part of modern-day Reality Television. Twenty-four hours a day, seven days a week, three hundred and sixty-five days a year there is a camera pointed in the direction of her desk. As with everything else she has undertaken, she is undaunted.

BC. Most people know this as a religious way of describing the years prior to one. SDP folks know this span of time as Before Cameras (which translates to 2012). An entirely new era arrived after their installation, thus creating "The Camera People." CPs are individuals from all over the world who, thanks to Explore.org, can get a glimpse into the Service Dog Project. They see the puppies being born, being fed, being trained, and just being dogs. Amazing how captivating something that sounds so simple can actually be.

I could not resist including this episode in regard to Cameras…
From the Doggie Daily---

Sunday, June 22, 2014
…THE TIME I THREW MY CLOTHES IN THE WASHING MACHINE AN GOT IN THE BATHTUB ONLY TO FIND OUT I HAD THROWN MY "I HAVE FALLEN AND I C

AN 'T GET UP " NECKLACE IN THE WASHING MACHINE AND THE TUMBLING HAD SET IT OFF. THIS MEANT I WAS IN THE BATH-- WITH 30 SECONDS TO GET TO THE "CALL BOX" AND PUSH A "NO THANK YOU "BUTTON--- WHILE IT WAS BLARING "MRS WHITE WE ARE CALLING THE EMERGENCY RESPONDERS FOR YOU"-- AT 76 YOU DO NOT JUST JUMP OUT OF THE TUB... BUT I GOT OUT AND RAN INTO THE KITCHEN TO PUSH THE "NO THANKS" BUTTON ONLY TO REMEMBER THE FIELD OF VIEW OF EXPLORE CAMERAS INCLUDED THAT BUTTON.

And then...
MEMORY HAS NEVER BEEN MY STRONG SUIT... BUT I DO REMEMBER ONE VERY EARLY EPISODE... A KNOCK ON THE DOOR (HAD TO BE A STRANGER-- NO ONE KNOCKS HERE) I GO ANSWER THE DOOR AND 2 VERY NICE WOMEN ARE STANDING THERE WITH A MOPS AND BUCKET-- THEY SIMPLY SAID "WE HAVE BEEN WATCHING THE CAMERAS AND IT LOOKS LIKE YOUR FLOOR COULD USE SOME MOPPING"

ABSOLUTELY-- YOU GO RIGHT AT IT.!!!

THEY CAME REGULARLY FOR ABOUT 6 MONTHS-- BROUGHT THEIR OWN BUCKET AND SOAP.... ... BLESS THEM...

ONLY

You need to know more about Carlene's 'Doggie Daily' (DD). Every morning, somewhere between 4am and 7am, as far as this author can tell, Carlene lights up her computer screen and begins to write the DD, as it is referred to. Early every morning she sends out the Doggie Daily (DD) newsletter, which may contain anything from commentary on a recent trip to the hardware store, to cameras in nursing homes, to thoughts on why she is, in fact, one of those folks who like dogs better than people. The most recent one I read included the following topics: toilet seats, duct tape, taxes, lid lowering, city life, guinea hens, annual calendars, postage, Hershey's moving to Mexico, unemployment, and salmonella. The diversity keeps you reading them, even in their raw form, a stream of consciousness with typos, misspellings and random punctuation. White does not have (or choose to take) the time to correct them. "Interpret them as you will," is the mantra I have heard from her, and the interpretations probably do vary. Her brain works a little faster than her fingers, and often when she is simply reaching for the 'a' key that damn pinky finger strikes the 'caps lock' and the result is exactly that, until another 'a' is required and turns it back off. Her left hand is slightly faster than her right and thus results in 'teh' rather than 'the' a huge majority of the time. This particular peculiar typo never fails to make me smile. At one point in time she discussed the continuing struggle of 'teh vs the' and has decided against even trying to rectify the situation. Enough said.

When Carlene and I were first brainstorming this book and what it was to be (which perhaps we have never completely agreed upon…) she asked her DD followers if we should utilize the original format/spelling/style of those emails or edit them into proper English. Here is our favorite reply to that question. From a very dedicated supporter, Carole.

September 8, 2019
MAY I VOTE TO KEEP YOUR ORIGINAL SPELLING IN THE DD'S? AS AN OLD FIRST GRADE TEACHER OF 41 YEARS (YEARS OF TEACHING NOT YEARS OF AGE. I'M 78) I USED TO LOVE THE INVENTED SPELLING OF THE CHILDREN. I REFUSED TO RED MARK THEIR PAPERS WHEN THEY WERE JUST LEARNING TO WRITE ON THEIR OWN.

SINCE A LOT OF US WHO WATCH AND LEARN HERE ARE OF A CERTAIN AGE, I THINK IT'S GOOD, HEALTHY PRACTICE FOR US TO INTERPRET YOUR SPELLING AND WORK OUT WHAT YOU MEAN. KIND OF LIKE DOING CROSSWORD PUZZLES AND SUDOKU.   YOUR SPELLING IS SUCH A CHARMING PART OF YOU. WE ALL KNOW WHAT A GENIUS YOU ARE SO ONLY VERY SMALL-MINDED PEOPLE WOULD JUDGE YOUR SPELLING.

Ah! Only small-minded people would judge us on our spelling and/or punctuation! As long as we are passionate and get the point across, all is forgiven. Excellent that the rules are not as stringent as they once were. Or perhaps it's just that there are exceptions to (nearly) every rule.

"She's ONLY a dog trainer." A brother-in-law described her to a stranger as "only a dog trainer. According to this redundant recollection, that is the very moment that the Service Dog Project was conceived. It took her twenty-five years to say (to him) "Just you wait a minute-- SKIP THAT "ONLY" PART.... I am a dog trainer -- a very good dog trainer."

"Only. What an insult, really, isn't it?" she inquires during one of our conversations. That question was rhetorical, and then she continues, "Have you ever been called 'Only a woman?' Or 'only' this or 'only' that?" she asks me sharply, peering through glasses that have one lense held in place with a strip of clear scotch tape. "Oh yes," I responded, "Oh yes I have." Those type of comments have always resonated with me as they do with her. Carlene and I have both been operators of businesses and in charge of many things, and we have both been overlooked by someone in our domain searching for the 'man in charge'. Just writing this raises my pulse and the pressure of the blood in my veins.

Here's the official story about ONLY from the Doggie Daily—

November 18, 2019
NEGATIVE NEST--- I THINK I JUST COINED THAT PHRASE- AND IT IS A DESCRIPTIVE ONE - DIDN'T SOMEONE WRITE A CHILDRENS NOVEL ABOUT THE SKY IS FALLING???? EVERY ONCE IN A WHILE SINCE WE HAVE HAD CAMERAS INSTALLED IN 2012 AND BEGAN TO BUILD SDP AS A VIRTUAL COMMUNITY OF INTERESTING PEOPLE.....- SOMEONE WILL GET A NEGATIVE IDEA--- AND A COUPLE PEOPLE WILL RUN WITH IT.... BUILDING A NEGATIVE NEST

TEH CREATIVITY OF SOME OF THESE PEOPLE IS INCREDIBLE- BELLA AND GEORGE-- WHAT A GREAT STORY----- DID I NOT GET "WHAT ARE YOU DOING ABOUT ALL THE KIDS YOU ARE NOT HELPING?" TEH ONLY ANSWER "NOTHING" BY DEFINITION-- THAT CAN GET SOMEONE OFF ON A NEGATIVE " SDP ONLY

HELPS ONE PERSON AT A TIME" NEXT THING YOU GET
A NEST OF PEOPLE WHO HAVE JUST BEEN WAITING
TO BUILD A NEGATIVE NEST OF LIKE MINDS...

WELL LETS UNLOAD TEH "ONLY" SDP DOES HELP ONE
PERSON AT A TIME..that #$%^&*word "only" has a history in
my life-- and the life of most women my age... **only a woman**-
- i know alot of stories on that one.

I CAN REMEMBER----(HERE WE GO---THIS WILL BE A
LONG-- touchy--- ONE--) SITTING WITH SISTER AND
BROTHER IN LAW, A PRIVATE PILOT,   IN A RESTAURANT
BOOTH- WE GOT TO TALKING ABOUT FLYING WITH OR
AGAINST TEH WIND.- START WITH -- I KNEW NOTHING
ABOUT IT-- WHICH NEVER STOPPED ME FROM
ARGUING- HE PROBABLY QUITE RIGHTLY SAID YOU GO
FASTER WITH PREVAILING WINDS.. ME... WITH ZERO
FLYING KNOWLEDGE-- SAID "THAT LIGHT AIRCRAFT
AROUND TEH WORLD FLIGHT WENT FROM EAST TO
WEST" WHICH STArrted a very loud arguement- because
with all his knowledge-- which was considerable-- all i had to
say was "they went my way"====== the volume of the
"discussion " was so intense that the man inthe next booth
stood up and said " what are you ? two aeronautical
engineeers??" and my brother in law said "SHE'S ONLY A
DOG TRAINER "-- it took me 25 years to say "just you wait a
minute-- SKIP THAT "ONLY" PART....   i am a dog trainer -- a
very good dog trainer"   AND BUOYED UP BY GEROGE
BUSH SENIOR'S "IF YOU CAN'T HELP THOUSANDS, HELP
ONE" - AND SDP WAS OFF AND RUNNING.

DAMN WORD "ONLY"
■■

You will read about a TED talk later in the book and that
gentleman states very clearly how much better multi-taskers
women are than men. At the risk of generalizing, many women
have that attribute, and certainly is not our ONLY one. Some

people are comfortable admitting to these things, and some people are not. I say, if you cannot talk about your own accolades, no one else is going to, either.

Prior to agreeing to write this documentary, I opened the Doggie Daily emails only occasionally, when I had time. Now I am hooked, wondering what is next on Carlene's mind to wonder about, examine, and solve. DDs are used primarily to communicate what is happening on a daily basis. Locally folks read it to see what tasks and volunteers may be needed that day, globally for such events as puppies, matches and fundraisers. So they do both; sprinkle in some observations, some facts, lots of truth, and a whole lot of strong opinions that are generally supported by at least one interesting story, sometimes from decades ago, and the result is your Doggie Daily. Sign up on the website! If you are reading this book you will not be disappointed and may even get a couple of extra conversations pieces to boot. Somewhere around eleven hundred people every day click on the email and open it, and a couple hundred more open it sometime after the first day, raising the statistic to around fifty percent. Two hundred or so more read the blog on a regular basis. That's a whole lot of people interested in what is going in at the Service Dog Project, and a much higher percentage than is achieved by many Constant Contact lists.

To Set Stage, A sample from Carlene, "Just in case you think I make up these stories...."

From the Doggie Daily—

Thursday, January 23, 2020
 To set the crazy acres stage (for the book) I was trying to refresh my memory and wrote to tommy Nugent   --- who was (and in my mind, still is   a 17 year old kid) who was thrilled with race horses, worked in our barn, and i was terrified he would get too involved with the race "trackers" and not take advantage of the super brain he obviously had-- he is now dr.nugent, who once studied endorphins in Kentucky.. to

whom we gave the Dane "Cuba"

I asked him… do I remember a horse in my basement??   His answer…..

Cheers to you and very nice to hear from you:

Yes, the racehorse in your basement was "Gal Friday." She was a filly we all loved. Kind and pretty and very nice and comfortable to ride. I loved that filly. You gave me a picture of her as a foal for Xmas one year with her mother..1972?

We took her out of the barn and put her in the warm basement because she had a fever and was sick and we were doing all we could to help her. The weather was severely cold and the vet suggested it. We didn't expect the rain, but despite the ankle deep water, she did just fine and recovered.

I hope you will edit this so as to not incriminate any of us, but I have a lot of memories of Chestnut Street. I believe you and Lynn Cashman once somehow came home with a fire hydrant.

I also recall being stopped with you by North Reading, MA Police for expired plates in 1972. The renewal stickers were clipped to the lamp in the kitchen. I was 17 and you were teaching me how to drive a horse trailer. (You did a good job. I still remember and can drive anything). As I recall, you had 3 or 4 wrist watches on each arm, to be repaired, and a tv or two in the back seat in the middle of a crime wave involving horse trailers and tv's. I forget who got us out of that.

When you mention the pet pig, I want to remind you of how she came to be. I had a little green MGB sports car, of which I was very proud. You gave me a big jar of penny's one day and sent me up Rt 128 to the hog farm and told me to ask the farmer if he would trade a piglet for their weight in pennies. He said yes and that little piglet sat on my lap all the way home and we became friends forever. She did become big, though. and was a hit in the circus the kids put on that summer .

Cuba was my best friend for a long time

Over and Out....Tommy Nugent

----

now that he mentions it... that story about the watches was very funny-- the police stopped us-- no sticker- tommy driving.
 i had been working on the remnants of my parents house and the jewelery box.... there was an accumulation of watches- so rather than stick them in my pocket, i put them on and wound them up to see which ones were working... so when the policeman stopped us....and finished with the paperwork of ticketing us, it was just too perfect, --- i pulled up my sleeve and said "you wanna buy a watch?"- there was some confusion after that--

-----

and i also remember the fire hydrant—we still have it   when i go in that shopping mall to this day, i remember that hydrant with the 4 foot of heavy iron pipe attached...both being horse people and accustomed to lifting 100 pound bags of grain-- lynn and i struggled with that thing- finally getting in our vehicle the whole time wondering if they had a surveillance camera--

---

i hope tommy continues to remind me of stuff for the daily doggie – I can call them nugent's nuggets. And I do.

28

TRAINING PEOPLE

"We're not training the dog; we are training the person," Carlene tells me adamantly. "These Danes are half trained when they are born! Don't wreck 'em—people wreck 'em! No one else looks from the standpoint of the dogs. It has its own way of looking at things. Can you imagine how that dog feels when asked to sit or fetch for no apparent reason?" She has raised her eyebrows at me over breakfast, an expression I have quickly learned means that I should be taking notes, which I am.

She then refers me to Sir Ken Robinson, who has sixty-four million views of his TED Talks about creativity and education. In general, TED celebrates the gift of the human imagination, and the talks are often thought-provoking. As soon as I am able to get online, I listen to the session she has recommended.

Mr. Robinson's presentation is captivating. "We are educating people out of their creativity." He tells the crowd, exasperated. "All kids have tremendous talents, capacities for innovation, and we squander them, pretty ruthlessly. A little girl, who, according to the teacher, rarely paid any attention in class, was drawing a picture of God and the teacher told her, "But nobody knows what God looks like." And the girl said, "They will in a minute."

He goes on with these thoughts, "We make very poor use of our talents. Education dislocates very many people (and animals) from their natural talents. Resources in people are buried deep, and you have to go looking for them. You might imagine that education (or 'training') is how that happens but it is not. Everybody has an interesting education…(however) we have bought into conformity."

Creativity is as important as literacy, and should be treated as such.   Carlene's interpretation is thought-provoking: education should be about passion, about what excites the brain to learn. These Danes can develop their own solutions. They should be allowed their creativity, their freedoms. When you put a vest on a service dog, you can see the passion, the desire to serve. It feeds their spirit, their energy, their happiness. And then, when the harness comes off, the Dane rests. With freedom and creativity, they are better at what they do. Better at life. The dog's intuition is utilized to make them better service dogs. SDP does not change how they think.

In addition, most people do not appreciate what the dogs already know. Carlene explains that, "There is a reason I received the Massachusetts Veterinarian Association's Award for *Improving the Human-Animal Connection*. We are educating the dog. Let me reiterate, we are training the person. We are educating the dog. They understand so much more than you think they do. My dogs don't want to retrieve! They look at you like you're crazy. Why would you throw something away and then think I should bring it back? What a waste of time, they are thinking. Why would you make me do something that doesn't have a purpose, that doesn't make any sense? They study you, wondering about your motivations. I swear they do. They are born knowing half of what we think they need to 'learn.' And they 'learn' so many things on their own, without any guidance from us. Watch the videos of these dogs walking their people down and up sets of stairs, across a creek full of rocks, wherever it may be, a crowded subway, a concert hall. They already know what needs to be done."

From the Doggie Daily—

December 14, 2015
We had some friends over for dinner which was nice. George loved the extra attention. Bella taught our friend why George didn't know how to sit on command. She didn't understand why a service dog wouldn't know how to sit. Bella explained it to her saying if George knew how to sit and some random person asked him to sit while she was using him for support she would fall backwards on her back and that wouldn't be very good. She then showed her how if she needs to get George down how she will ask him to down and he will slowly lower and sometimes will help lower Bella on his way down. But it was a cool piece of information for someone who assumes all dogs should know how to sit. But how in George's case him not knowing how to sit on command is a protection for Bella. That was about the excitement of our night. Thanks for looking in on us and have a wonderful night.
 Love Bella and George

The puppies are always fed in the office/living room, each with their own bowl, their own space. There is no fighting for food or territory. As another exercise the dedicated people here feed them by name, with a spoon, so that they learn patience, and attention, and the importance of both. They are incredibly observant, you may look at these Danes and think they are not paying attention, and I guarantee that is not the case. Especially when they get their service vests on, they absolutely pay attention. Carlcne explains it to me this way, "Are they being too rough? Slow them down, surprise them, change the behavior. These Danes look at you and ask 'what are you going to teach me next?' What you do, what you say, does not go unnoticed. These dogs just learn. There is no force. They understand so much more than most people think they do."

This section comes directly from Carlene on training, which is clearly one of her favorite topics, her passion, her expertise. *"Please note," she begins, "—my opinions here are mine and are just suggestions about dog training in general. There are hundreds of service dogs that could well deserve national attention of an AKC award, however our Great Dane "George" was chosen. It had a lot to do with the fact that his partner is a 48- pound cute little girl who now walks because of George. Thereby wags a tail/TALE…*

My introduction to an official service dog training group was "you Great Dane people are nuts",---- I hope I have not failed to deliver on that one.

For a variety of reasons, we now have donated over 200 Great Dane balance dogs to put people back on the feet walking. The part which I think bears some study, is that our strange training gets these Great Danes fully trained, (or preferably educated) passing all Assistance Dog International (ADI) Tests and out thinking and working in the real life by the time they are one-year-old. Could this process be used with labs and goldens? I DUNNO.

This is a very subtle thing, but we try never to use our muscles to control the dog even as a very young pup. We do not pick them up and carry them around ... unless absolutely necessary. We persuade them to follow us – or come sit on our lap as we sit on the floor
Our reason being if we have had to pick them up, then we are having to force them to do something they might not want to do. Better to ask them. Never tighten a leash- that is a conversation tool.

We start their "PREPARATION FOR TRAINING" by the time they are 3 weeks old, when they have nursed for a bit, so they are not very hungry, we introduce one pup to one dish of a goat's milk/ground up puppy food gruel. We would never shove their face in the food but we assist with a spoon, --a lift and lick operation-- until they understand there is a bowl of food there somewhere. They often put one foot in to be sure.

By 4 weeks they are eating out of their individual bowls very nicely. After they have had a meal, so they are not starving, we serve desert- some canned food-, BY SPOON -- one at a time, say their name and serve the food, very soon because there is no competition for food, if we hesitate, the pup will naturally sit and look up waiting for more food to appear, and it does. The trick now is to produce the spoonful exactly when the butt hits the ground.

By 5 weeks we can add pups so there are 2 or 3 pups sitting waiting. By 6 weeks 5-8 pups with no excitement, they know what is expected, sit and wait.

The COVER photo shows the whole litter of Great Dane pups sitting perfectly waiting for their own spoonful AT 7 WEEKS OF AGE –Interestingly the one not paying attention is the 100% white/ deaf who is still here and a very well trained model in commercials.

At that point it is possible to take the entire litter out for a walk *controlled only with a can of food and a spoon, tapping the can will tell them all to fall in line and we go for a walk around stopping every once in a while for a sit down and snack. We talk to them, we do not give commands, they listen carefully for that slight tap of the spoon on the can, which eventually becomes a very quite "come on gang, pay attention" we can then swap from spoon and can to small biscuits. The biscuits are used only rarely… and never as "typical training treats" -- ONLY AT END OF SESSION TYPE TREAT…*

Once we have absolute control over the entire litter, we start to break it up, introduce a leash, which is never tightened; a couple of tugs and immediately release. We talk to them constantly; the two tugs on the leash for attention is left over from the two taps on the can, "hey listen to me and think."

By five months, the harness "on" becomes a switch to work mode. "Get in the car and go somewhere" to look at new things while walking exactly the speed of the person by whom they are handled. Add a few elevators, shopping carts and very critically the one step on the stairs, up and down, plus the rest of generic life with consistence and strict obedience to harness on and off rules. By the time they are seven months old they are beginning to look and act like a serious dog at least when in harness, take that harness off, feed them a few treats and they will roar around like a normal kid when school lets out. By a year old when the harness is on, they are looking and thinking about who's feet are where and why. They are ready to work.

During this time, they have basically lived in and around the various kennels and fields. We do let volunteers take them for occasional overnights but we do not want the pups to become too attached to any one person. We do not go along with the puppy raiser concept. In my experience a dog can sometimes spend the rest of their lives looking for the persons who raised them. The "oh how happy they are to see you" seems often to be "finally you are back in my life, can we really go home now?" Then when they don't the tail drops in submission and the joy is gone.

When we start an applicant, we put the person in our guesthouse with cookies and watch what happens. Most often the dog decides this is the person they have been waiting for and in 24 hours they become bonded. The dog is "behaving" with normal conversation. A few days of working with the dog in real life situations and the team is certified by SDP. No dog leaves our driveway until they will follow the person all over, away from their friends and trainers, without a leash. They have to love to work.

There are a few concepts to discuss. One very primary lesson is that we rarely use our muscles to "control" a Dane, this is called "plan ahead" because eventually they will out weigh most handlers anyway. We talk to them, we never drag them around with a tight leash, and we never give out treats when we are actually teaching them to work. Once the harness is on: no treats, lots of praise and no free time. The harness is a switch on and off duty. A normal chain training collar and 24-inch leash is what is used. The dog in harness is immediately next to their handler, never wandering.

Many taller Danes are not known for their physical courage so another critical aspect is they have a play yard which involves stairs, with open backing, ramps, rocking horses and mannequins to get them used to someone standing still staring at them. Their sleeping quarters involve either steps or a ramp to a raised sleeping loft with bedding. It is much warmer in their lofts; they can see out windows and they get practice climbing the stairs to get there.

We breed our own style of Danes, which are shorter and heavier than the typical show Dane. The concept is best explained by comparing a basketball player to a football player. We need the football-player-type Danes for balance work. There is an old Amish saying that "in a work animal the leg should be one-half the height."

35

We do not breed related Danes, and often import new bloodlines from European kennels. I realize' pride goeth before a fall,' but we have had less than 1% hip dysplasia or bloat in about 450 pups since I started this in 2003. Regarding age, the three dogs I put out in 2004 needed to be replaced in 2014, after having worked for ten years. My oldest dog was fourteen and the white dog I had at my first ADI conference was thirteen years old when she slept. We have had a few earlier deaths for specific causes like cancer.

We have also had hundreds of requests nationwide for a Dane service dog since Bella and George hit ABC News in 2015; we cannot help them. I hope other training facilities consider adding Danes to their student population. Please watch this video- three of our dogs with children.
https://youtu.be/w6wd53xHEfc

From the Doggie Daily—

October 11, 2014
WE START OUR EDUCATION WITH SPOON FEEDING -- CALLING THEM ALL PUPPY PUPPY PUPPY -- THEN CALLING BY NAME -- WHICH IS PURELY TO TEACH THEM ALL THIS NOISE WE MAKE HAS MEANING. AND WE GO ON WITHOUT LEASH AND COLLAR FOR A VERY LONG TIME. WE TRY NOT TO USE OUR MUSCLES TO CONTOL THEM… THEY GET TO A STATE OF READY TO LEARN--- THEY EVEN LOOK AT YOU DIFFERENTLY…
 AND YOU CAN MOVE ON WITH GAMES.. GETTING UP ON TABLES/RAMPS/INTO CARS --- WAIT TIL TOLD TO EAT THIER FOOD... LIE DOWN FOR A FEW SECONDS...PLAY IN THE ARENA JUST NONSENSE THINGS. LEARNING TO COMMUNICATE...

 AND THEN THEY LEARN WHAT QUARTERHORSE PEOPLE CALL "THE RULE OF THE ROPE" IT IS ABSOLUTE... DON'T FIGHT IT -- DON'T EVEN TIGHTEN IT. WHEN IT IS ON ... PAY ATTENTION. THEY MUST BEHAVE-- WITHOUT QUESTION.

AND YOU ARE WELL ON YOUR WAY TO A WELL
EDUCATED DOG.

THE TYPICAL "OBEDIENCE TRAINED DOG" CERTAINLY
JUMPS TO ATTENTION ON COMMAND,
AND SOMEONE TOLD ME THAT THE PUPPY RAISED
 DOG FOR THE SEEING EYE PROGRAM HAS TO KNOW
39 COMMANDS AT 18 MONTHS , AS THE START THIER
OFFICIAL TRAINING.... THE SEEING EYE CERTAINLY
TURNS OUT EXTREMELY USEFUL AND WELL TRAINED
DOGS-- I THINK YOU WILL NOTICE NONE OF THEM ARE
DANES...

DANES JUST DON'T HAVE THAT WORK ETHIC... BUT AT
18 MONTHS DANES ARE USUALLY OUT DOING WHAT
THEY DO BEST.. HELPING THEIR PARTNERS WALK...
■■■

September 11, 2019
I HAVE SEEN SEVERAL OF TEH TRAINERS AND
WALKERS NOT GIVING THE DOGS A COOKIE WHEN
THEY GET IN THE CAR...

SOUNDS LIKE "WHAT'S TEH FUSS?"" WELL WE START
THAT WHEN WE ARE ASKING THEM TO GET BACK IN
THEIR KENNEL-- THEY SHOULD READILY GO IN,, TURN
AROUND.. AT WHICH TIME THEY GET A COOKIE...
AS THEY BECOME SERVICE DOGS... THAT SIMPLE
ROUTINE BECOMES JUMP IN THE CAR AND TURN
AROUND TO GET A COOKIE....---- AND GET YOUR TAIL
OUT OF THE WAY
THIS BECOMES ONE OF THOSE SIMPLE THINGS WHICH
MAKE LIFE WITH A DANE EASIER...AS IT RUNS OVER
INTO GOING THRU THE DOOR TO THE MALL-- GO THRU
WHEN TOLD TO --- TURN AROUND AND GET BACK TO
WORK IN LINE.-- SIMPLE THINGS;.

ALSO WHAT I CALL "BULK MANAGEMENT" THE VERY SIZE OF THESE DOGS MEANS YOU DO NOT WANT THEM JUMPING AROUND CONFUSED... LIKE WANDA... THE JACK RUSSELL.   THEY MUST LEARN... EARLY IN TH EGAME... THINGS LIKE WHOA-- STAND STILL- OK JUMP IN.. BACK UP- ARE ALL CRITICAL FOR BULK MANAGEMENT.

■■

October 11, 2014
FACT-- I AM STILL CONVINCED THE PART THAT IS LACKING FROM MOST "TRAINING METHODS" IS BEST ILLUSTRATED BY THE OLD MOVIE "MIRACLE WORKER"----- PATTY DUKE PLAYS HELEN KELLER- BORN BLIND AND DEAF- AN IMPOSSIBLY FRUSTRATED AND VIOLENT CHILD UNTIL SHE FIGURES OUT THAT THOSE HAND MOVEMENTS MEAN "WATER". I HAVE SEEN SOOOO MANY DOGS WHO JUST DON'T UNDERSTAND THE BASICS...

AS FOR THEIR ABSOLUTE BEHAVIOR WHEN IN HARNESS.... A PERFECT EXAMPLE YESTERDAY--- I WENT TO "BED AND BATH"-- FIRST TIME IN A REAL STORE IN MAYBE A YEAR.... I HAD LOST MY GRANNY FORK--- A SMALL 2 TINED - WOOD HANDLED FORK-- PERGECT FOR STICKING IN A BAKED POTATO TO TEST IF IT IS DONE.... OR A RUMP ROAST TO CARVE IT....

I HAD BENTLEY WITH ME-- I AM GETTING TO THE POINT OF NEEDING HIM---AT LEAST TO GET TO A SHOPPING CART... AS WE WANDERED PAST THE 15 FOOT HIGH DISPLAY OF CARVING KNIVES, HE HESITATED EVER SO SLIGHTLY, WHICH CAUGHT MY EYE…INSTEAD OF "COMMANDING HIM TO WALK ON" I
 CHECKED...LUCKILY... HIS HARNESS HAD HOOKED THE METAL ON THE DISPLAY OF THE 15 FOOT HIGH COLLECTION OF KNIVES... IF HE HAD WALKED ON, HE WOULD HAVE EASILY TOPPLED THE ENTIRE THING. I

SAW- AND GAVE THE ULTIMATE COMMAND "WHOA" AND
HE FROZE.
GOOD BOY...
"WHOA" IS A BIGGIE IN OUR WORLD...
■■

Friday, November 17, 2017
discombobulated ramble today......what happened??? we
have a surplus of people and not enough who can train dogs...
i wish i had a nickle for every phone call i get about training
dogs in general-- if i then had another nickle for the number of
calls i get abotu providing an "emotional support dog" we
would not have to worry about selling chicken bricks.... there
is something lacking in the basic understanding of animals--
maybe it comes from 2 parents working to put food on the
table--(mind you, food is one of my personal favorite
things)..... but in an effort to provide animal experience,
parents take the least labor intensive way out and buy a
hamster which they keep all alone in a nice tidy cage- or a
canary-with no regard for the social life of the solitary animal..
and the kid involved learns a feed/water/ detachment to the
mind of the beast... it is that detachment that ends someone
on the phone saying "i bought this puppy, i need to have you
train it for me to have as a companion" what i want to say is
 try taking care of it yourself and thinking about some other
 living thing will start you on what you need anyway...
 Mo (a rescue mule), all 1800 pounds of her- arrived here
mad at people-- and kicking...kicking with authority at anyone
within reach...then we turned her loose in the yard-- no more
kicking, great interest in bud's various projects in the shop--
many people can not get over the personality she has
developed... all on her own… we just let her…

so many dogs are micromanaged-- leash laws mean never a
chance to run unless there is a dog park - and someone
willing to take them there... how m any dogs i have watched ...
on a leash.. trying to move their bowels while being dragged
along by someone half awake, totally detached from what is

39

happening....the norm "buy a cute pup.. get a collar to drag it around... feed it good food til it gets stronger than you and drags you around- so you give it up as impossible" .   when... in soooo many cases having a well trained dog means merely to teach the owner how to graciously cope with another living thing. it is not micro managing a mechanical robot...

maybe half of our "program' is allowing the dog to bond with their new partner-- which is why i still question the accepted process of giving a puppy to a puppy raiser, then taking it back at over a year old - usually into a crate in a training facility for months, -- then giving it to work for someone-- when it is possible the dog is still looking for it's puppy raiser...
giving up for the day...

Oct 6 2017
"HI--- i am calling because my doctor says i should have a service dog"
  when ye olde md does not have a clue what a service dog is or does... and chances are a normal dog would do alot for most people... at least get them out in the fresh air for a few minutes a day !!
now for.... in my opinion...
 so you wanna get a dog??? please for 6 seconds, give some thought as to what the breed was bred to do... because some things are counterproductive to modern civilization...for example-- if throwing yellow tennis balls is something you always wanted to do... then the labs and goldens are your dog. and a dane is not.. the lab will go get the ball , pick it up , and proudly carry it back to where you stand... the dane may just watch you throw it... or maybe even run to where it is and put his foot on it... proud of the fact that he located it for you.. so you know where to come get it yourself. historically... the lab was used to retrieve a fallen- shot- bird so you can take it home for dinner. the dane was bred to chase wild boar- and not kill, but just run around it and create enough confusion so someone else could come and do it in... sound familiar?

now if you want to track a lost child in the woods... a
bloodhound would put his sophisticated   nose to the ground
and if you learn the dog language , he could tell you all sorts
of things. with a dane,,,, you could drop a piece of steak on
the ground in front of him... and he coud not find it.----- do not
be surprised if a border collie chases cars-- or anything that
moves.... or a jack russell that alerts you to th ef act that the
trash people are picking up your neighbors trash.
then the biggie of all this... do not be surprised if you have a
dog with those huge jaw muscles boxers,.. pit bulls...
bulldogs... if they bite things.. that is what they are bred to
do... bite and hang on while their smushed in nose allows
them to breathe.--- thy may not be mean and aggressive, they
love to bite-- a happy game with them...
there are other "givens" -- you can not walk a beagle in the
woods without a good leash... because one sniff of a rabbit
and you will listen to his excited bark as he follows the rabbit
for miles.....oblivious of you... somewhat like the sight
hounds... grey hounds etc.. one glimse of a deer and they are
gone.
german shephards are serious workers...not inclined to be the
goofy entertainment of a toy poodle.... but happier working...

41

Carlene on trained Great Danes…."Guess which dog is a dane and which a jack russel terrier in trying to photo this "calendar shot" in the snow…"

Bentley... come here on this tobaggan
here?
right--- good boy
wanda… come here
OHAHUMANHASCALLEDMYNAMEIGETEXCITEDWHENAN
YONECALLSMYNAMEITISSUCHANICESOUNDTOOTHATM
EANSICAN THEN
RUNOVERANDJUMPINTHEIRLAPANDWAGMYTAILATTHE
RESTOFTHEWORLD. "
wanda ---just stand there
IAMSOHAPPYTOSTANDTHEREBUTICANALSOJUSTSTAN
DONTHREEFEET"
Opal… now you sit here
ok
wanda get back there
"IAMSOHAPPYTOSTANDTHEREBUTICANALSOJUSTSTAN
DONTHREEFEET"

Wanda put that foot down

"HOWCANIPUTTHATFOOTDOWNWHENIAMSUREISAWAC
HIPMUNKDARTINTOTHATHOLEANDTHEREISSSOMEONE
OVERTHEREI HAVENOTSEEN
BEFOREANDMUSTTALKTOANDWHYMUSTIHAVE4FEETO
NTHEGROUNDWHENICANSTANDVERYNICELYWITH3BUT
AS SOONASYOUSAYTHEMAGICWORDOF "OK "
 IWILLZOOMAROUNDTOTHATNEWPESONANDTHENJUMP
INSOMEONESLAPANDRELAX"

"wanda stop turning around.

"IJUSTHADTOTURNAROUNDANDSEEWHOTHATDOGWAS
BEHINDMESEEINGASHEIS20TIMESMYSIZEIANDTOBESU
REICANSTILLWHIPHIM
OHITISONLYADANEANDIKNOWICANBOSSTHEMAROUND
DIDYOUWANTMYTAILUPORDOWNICANWAGITSIDETOSID
EIAMSOHAPPPYTOBEHERECHECKINGOUTTHESECURIT
YOFTHEPLACE ANDICANTELLTHATTHENEED FOR
MYSERVICES
ISGREATBECAUSEIAMSURETHEREAREALSOSQUIRRELS
AROUNDLETMEATHIM."

October 8, 2017

i would love to have more people get into dane training... the
danes are such naturals... and a perfectly trained dane is
sooooo spectacular... stands out in the crowd... i wish teh
great dane club of america would acknowledge george-- and
wendy ....

most of the "show" dane community wants nothing to do with
me-- i offended a few at an early age by buying 100 blue
ribbons from the ribbon maker for 15 cents each and avoiding
all the hassles of dog showing-- my dogs were better than
nearly everyone else's---- in my opinion... unfortunately my
opinion was not shared by most of the show world..

 i remember the guy/ veteran, in teh wheelchair with a whit
westie small dog.... at the ΛDI (Assistance Dogs International,
we are an accredited member of this organization) convention
" first they blow my legs off me, then they give me this ladies

lap dog.. i want one of yours." there is nothing like a Dane for service work... (He got one…)

"This one gentleman Veteran had anger problems, had been to counseling, had tried to solve it, many times, many ways. I gave him a dog, because of these problems. They said I put that dog in danger. Well, I would never do that! That dog is fine, and he will be fine. I would have shot the guy had he put my dog in danger! I don't care that much about the guy."

As I was researching different sources for this book, I sent out a quick questionnaire to the folks who were interested in being included. One of the questions was simply this: Who needs more training, the person or the dog? Hands down, people's answer that question was the person. Every time.

Via email a few days later I received sad news from Carlene. "One of the pups died, and I need to get everyone past that. It was a good pup." As always, short and to the point. She realized, they all realized, that the pup could have changed someone's life, made it better, had it survived. "Sh*t happens," she writes to me, brushing it off, moving on, pretending nonchalance. There is no nonchalance when it comes to her dogs. None. They are far more important than people. Better at judging characters. More loyal. More predictable. More intuitive. Nicer.

I was watching 5pm Mail Call last evening and there was a conversation between Carlene and one of her employees in regard to a dog that could not be seen, off camera. Carlene had pointed and said, "That's a good dog." And there was a bit of uncertainty visible in the employee, as though she doubted that particular animal. "That's a good dog," Carlene repeated, and what she was saying was, "They are all good, when given the proper opportunity." Perhaps that point cannot be emphasized enough. She is certainly not 'only' a dog trainer.

DASH & SCOTT

"Scott is the only person I ever ran a background check on. Cost me $99. It wasn't good. My dog liked him. I took a risk. It paid off." –Carlene White via email interview March 2019. Scott was paired with Dash in January of 2015 and together they have accomplished great things.

From the Doggie Daily
November 13, 2017
i am still getting emails about Scott's video---
https://mountainlake.org/vch-turning-a-mess-into-a-message/
 polly suggested you all put it on your facebook pages-- sounds like a reasonable idea... he is doing a good job... (so is the dog....) I am more interested in the dog than the person, most times

He was lucky that he could not tie a proper knot---- and he was also lucky that i was not shocked by the fact he had a warrant out for his arrest. the reason i was not shocked... was i too have had a warrant to be arrested- a long story about a leash law violation, cocktail hour and not having $6.00 for bail.. but what it did do ... is that record will prohibit me from getting a top secret clearence again. i hope i don't need it ... as my job was to figure out how to bomb the united states most efficiently... i think what i determined is pretty much "what goes around comes around " and the fall out of a very few bombs will drift all the way round the world.... which should be detrimental to any bombing decision

I met Scott and Dash under the most interesting of circumstances, each of us helping a friend on a construction project, of all things…long story short Scott recruited me to write about their path, the "Mess to the Message", and I was unable to resist! I drove across the North Country of New York State early one winter morning to hear Scott speak in a small high school library. What I heard there, what I saw there, stole my heart. Inspired me, motivated me, to be along be along on the journey of this man and his service dog. My life has not been the same since.

In his speeches and his life, Scott ties together a couple of interesting philosophies. The first; there are two important dates in your life, the one you are born on, and the one you die on. Between them is a dash. Make that dash, your time here on earth, as wonderful as it can possibly be.

The second philosophy: there are two days in your life that are the most important. The day you were born, and the day you figure out why. I firmly believe that Scott was born to carry his message to others, to prevent suicides and to make people feel as if they are not alone. He is a natural storyteller and even teenagers are transfixed. Silent. Listening. Hanging on every word, in fact. Every word.

The following excerpts are from Scott's Biography, *Knot Today*, in his own words.

It was when I was at the Uniformed Services Program I worked
with a woman who had a Great Dane named Wicked. I wasn't really
talking to the counselors, I was struggling. But when I would go into her office, with Wicked, she noticed I would open up more and more. So the counselors sat down as a team and decided that perhaps I should get a service dog.

I had nothing to lose so headed to Ipswich and the Service Dog Project to volunteer. While I was there I met Carlene White, the owner of the Project. She is perhaps a little cranky, she can be a little miserable, but, God love her, she lets you know where you stand with her right off the bat! Carlene and I got talking, and she told me what I needed to do; I needed to prove my dedication. To do this I would come down once a month, a five-hour drive for me, and when a few months passed they would look into pairing me with a dog. I did as she asked.

"Well since you are here for a few days we have a dog that we would love you to meet, a dog that needs a little help." Perfect for me, since I need a little help, too, I thought to myself at the time. Just one more thing I have in common with this Great Dane. And here comes Dash. She jumped up on the couch next to me, put her head on my shoulder with the biscuit in her mouth, and she dropped it in my lap. She chose me. She chose me! I took Dash for the weekend and returned Monday. Carlene sat me down and told me that she knew all about me. "I just want you to listen to me," she said, and not in a mean way. She's savvy. Very savvy.

These dogs are worth twenty-five thousand dollars so she is not willing to take the chance that someone is going to take these dogs, abuse them, sell them, whatever. She told me that she understood what I had gone through, and I appreciated that. She was upset that I had not told her the truth. Understandably so. With that, I could not apologize enough. She did not want my apologies, just honesty going forward, because, she explained, "My dog chose you. Who am I to judge my dog?" she asked me. "Here's what's going to happen. You are going to take her home and do good things with her. I want you to do something good with her, pay it forward somehow, some way." And with that we stood up and she gave me a hug. My views of Carlene changed completely. She wasn't quite as cranky as I had originally thought; in fact, that woman is amazing! Stern and straight with a heart of gold. She changed my life. Dogs are smarter than people some times, and more intuitive. Dash knew that I needed her, and in turn that I would take care of her. She has rarely left my side.

Scott continues to grow his resume and speaks frankly about his experiences, including an attempt at suicide, to our military, law enforcement, middle and high school students.

From the Doggie Daily—

December 23, 2019
THANKFULLY SCOTT WROTE A COMMENT FOR TH DD
TODAY....
Hello everyone
As we all know when I was paired with Dash, Carlene and I had a heart to heart and in words that only Carlene could use she told me "who am I to question my dog with her choosing you Scott, so take her and do good things with her, pay it forward."
So after a few years of paying it forward with Dash at my side in speaking to veterans, first responders, law enforcement, high schools, colleges and pretty much anyone who would benefit and listen to my presentations, I figured it was time to take it to the next level in my paying it forward (after all when Carlene said pay it forward she never told me when to stop). So here we are ......
I (we) are in the initial phases of creating a non profit organization which would enable us to broaden our spectrum of those who would benefit from our message. Benefit in the fact that they can take their mess and make it their message. In all of my travels and speaking to thousands there's always

been one common theme with those wanting help. And that's the cost of traveling. There are so many amazing organizations out there that so many people would benefit from but many can't afford the cost of traveling to them via airfare, ground cost and or lodging. That's where we are stepping in.

Our organization will sponsor travel costs to those who need to get to all these amazing accredited organizations such as but not limited to, The Service Dog Project, Homeward Bound Adirondacks, The Brattleboro Retreats Uniformed Services Program and oh so many more all over the United States. Again we are still in the developmental phase of this but we have focus, we have a large vision in helping others, and we have so many amazing people helping us in getting this done. As of right now the name will be 'Knot Today', the same as my book. After all, it got me to where I am today because it was not today for me with my lack of knot tying skills.

Please stay tuned for further updates in our mission. This is something that will forever serve those who served us.

Much love to all,

Scott and Dash

■■

Update—as of February 27, 2020 the 501c3 (non-profit) application has been accepted and is in process with the assorted governmental entities required, a Board of Directors is in place and *'Knot Today—Connecting Services to those who Served'* is underway. This program is how we can all potentially give back to those who risk their lives for our country and our well-being. We are confident that 'Knot Today' will be an excellent non-profit partner of the Service Dog Project by the middle of 2020. I am a member of the Board of Directors, Scott is the Executive Director and is absolutely at the helm of this, his latest challenge. www.ScottAubin.com

Knot Today is available on Amazon in both Ebook and paperback formats. A portion of the proceeds, of course, go to the SDP.

Scott and Dash, speaking at Dogfest 2019

RANDOM ACTS OF KINDNESS

The 19th of every month is *SDP Act of Kindness Day*. Carlene is a huge proponent of offering random acts of kindness with the understanding that people simply love to be appreciated. It is truly an admirable organizational philosophy, and falls into the category of uplifting every chance you get. I sincerely hope that LifeSaver's Inc. donates a pallet or two of their wonderful candy after I send them a copy of this book…

"Cake Day" specifically; cakes are delivered by volunteers to the local First Responders, firehouses mainly. There are now cakes donated in forty-seven of the fifty states each month. Here is a version of the flyer that accompanies each cake, delivered monthly to Fire Houses nationwide on the 19th, as a reward to those first responders who put their lives on the line every day, perhaps their own version of random acts of kindness.

Random Acts of Kindness –
Worldwide

by The Service Dog Project (SDP)

The local SDP fan who delivered your cake is part of a small worldwide army who follow the daily progress of SDP Great Dane service dogs thanks to the six explore.org cameras on the SDP farm in Ipswich, Massachusetts.

This SDP/explore.org community is extremely loyal and generous,
and supports SDP in so many ways,
including random acts of kindness –

like delivering cakes to First Responders.

How great is that? Time for cake!
Enjoy!

DEC 21 2017
I HAVE DECIDED I LIKE FIREMEN-- OF BOTH SEXES...
COURAGEOUS BUNCH OF BRIGHT PEOPLE SITTING
AROUND WITHOUT MUCH TO DO MOST OF THE TIME...
THIS GIVING THEM A "THANK YOU CAKE" ON THE 19TH
OF THE MONTH IS FUN FOR EVERYONE ! AND I LOVE TO
HEAR STORIES...

52

From the Doggie Daily—

February 21, 2019
Then.... the cake deal on the 19th---i was in the "big cake store"(not the supermarket kind) buying two artistic and delicious cakes- one for sdp-- the other for gerogetown fire deopt... who have come to expect it. standing around in teh store , a couple standing there heard me ask for a top whichsaid happy 19th - they asked why 2 cakes both appy 19th.. which gave me a chance to tell them about the fire departments getting cakes in42 states just on a whim.. they said they live close to the ipswich fire dept-- so I gave them a cake to take there-- they were a jolly couple a dn got right in the spirit of the nonsense.. then delivered mine to georgetown- - . and the guy was all smiles...
cheers everyone up.

Clearly other grateful Service Dog Recipients have been inspired by Carlene's Random Acts of Kindness:

From the Doggie Daily--

October 26, 2018
MORNING FROM NASHVILLE. IT HAS BEEN A YEAR AND A HALF SINCE I WAS HONORED TO BRING TUMBLER HOME TO BE PART OF OUR FAMILY. I NEVER THOUGHT THAT SHE WOULD DRAW SO MUCH ATTENTION EVERYWHERE WE TAKE HER. MOST OF THE COMMENTS ARE HOW BEAUTIFUL SHE IS AND AND HOW WELL BEHAVED SHE IS. SHE IS TOO WELL MANNERED TO LET IT GO TO WASTE. I AM IN PROCESS OF HAVING HER CERTIFIED TO BECOME A THERAPY DOG TO PLAY IT FORWARD. SHE BRINGS SO MANY SMILES TO FACES. I FEEL NURSING HOMES AND VANDERBILT CHILDRENS HOSPITAL COULD USE SOME REASON TO SMILE. I ENJOYED WATCHING DOGFEST. EVERYONE SEEMED TO HAVE A GRAND TIME. WHAT A JOYFUL COUPLE OF DAYS SEEING SO MANY RECIPIENTS IN ONE AREA TOGETHER WITH THEIR LIFE

CHANGING DOGS BY THEIR SIDE. NO OTHER PLACE ON
EARTH !!!!!!
PLAN ON HEADING UP THEIR FOR MY 7TH VISIT IN
APRIL !!!
HUGS TO ALL MY NORTHERN FRIENDS.
KARI J

September 13, 2015
I've been watching new puppies born at Service Dog Project
and just read a wonderful description posted by a visitor…I
love knowing I am a small but very important part of an
organization of WONDERFUL people who want nothing more
than to make life better for others. It restores my faith in
humankind to meet so many hard working, kind volunteers &
staff members, led by a woman who thinks out side the box.
Crazy Acres exudes love from all its pores and affects all
ages---and just enough sadness and loss to make the
wonderfulness more evident.
It is a place of respite and beauty.
The lives of many within the cyber community that is SDP
through Explore.org have been and will continue to be
enlightened many fold by giving enjoyment and allows even
the person farthest away to be a valuable part of the mission.
There is no effort or contribution "too small" to be important. I
will forever be thankful for finding and being welcome to
volunteer at SDP and feel pride in knowing I have a tiny part in
making the lives of 100+ recipients' easier and much more
enjoyable.

From the Doggie Daily

December 1, 2016
yesterday-- jane (new volunteer) decided to get teh visiting of
nursing homes bY OUR DOGS UNDEER
CONTROL......TERRIFFIC IDEA... THE PATIENTS AND THE
STAFF ARE ALWAYS CHEERED BY HAVING THE DOGS
DO A WALK THRU.... EVEN WITHOUT THE PAT THE
PUPPY ROUTINE... AND SHE RAN INTO WHAT IS MAYBE

54

THE CLOSEST ONE TO CRAZY ACRES... I WON'T
MENTION THE NAME BECAUSE THEY COULD SUE ME I
AM SURE FOR WHAT I THINK OF THAT OUTFIT.-- IT IS
THE CLOSEST THING TO A JAIL FOR SENIORS I CAN
THINK OF...
100 YEARS AGO IN THE PROCESS OF TRAINING DOGS
I USED TO WALK THRU- AND THEN THEY GOT A NEW
DIRECTOR WHO DECIDED I NEEDED TO HAVE NOT
ONLY A RABIES BUT MONTHLY STOOL SAMPLE
BEFORE I COULD EVEN WALK THRU--- AND I KNEW
SOME OF THE PATIENTS THERE SO I REALLY WANED
TO CONTINUE- AND OFFERED TO BRING THE CURRENT
LITTER OF PUPS TO RUN AROUND IN THE YARD
OUTSIDE THE WINDOWS SO THE PATIENTS COULD
ENJOY THE PUPS... AND WAS TOLD THE GUYS WHO
CUT THE GRASS DID NOT WANT THAAT TO HAPPEN..
EVEN AFTER I TOLD HIM I WOULD PICK UP ANYTHING
THAT FELL OUT OF THE PUPS.
 OK....

SKIP NOW TO CURRENT...JANE GOT THE IDEA OF
GOING THERE----NICE LOOKING BIG PLACE--- AND TEH
"DIRECTOR" TOLD HER TO BRING IN THE RABIES
CERTIFICATION... SO JANE GOT LINDA TO COPY THEM
AND SHE WENT BACK... AND WAS TOLD SHE ALSO
NEEDED THE OTHER VACINATION RECORDS - SO JANE-
BEING HONEST ANT THOROUGH-- GOT THE HEALTH
RECORDS SHOWING VACINES AND OFFERED TO BRING
THEM TO THE NURSING HOME OFFICE.... SO WE COULD
STOP BY WITH DOGS THAT DAY....
WELL... THIS DIRECTOR SAID SHE HAD MEETINGS AND
WOULD NOT BE ABLE TO LOOK AT THE PAPERWORK
TIL 4:30...
IT WAS SOUNDING DREADFULLY FAMILIAR.. JANE
NEEDED AN EDUCATION -- SO I DECIDED TO TAKE JANE
WITH DOGS TO THE
NURSING HOME THT BRINGS THE PEOPLE HERE IN A
BUSS EVERY SO OFTEN...

I SAID I DOUBTED WE NEEDED ANY PAPERWORK, AND WITH DOGS UNDER 100% CONTROL, THEY WOULD WELCOME US WITH OPEN ARMS -- WHICH THEY DID... AND PLEASE COME BACK ANY TIME.. THE RESIDENTS LOVE THE DOGS AND THE VISIT AND WHAT A WONDERFUL   BLAH BLAH BLAH...

WE HAD FUN... THE DOGS HAD FUN...THE PEOPLE HAD FUN AND THE STAFF WAS THRILLED. SO I SUGGESTED TO JANE SHE FOLLOW THRU WITH THE WAY THE RESIDENTS WERE TREATED IN BOTH HOMES....THERE IS A STORY TO BE TOLD-- INFORTUNATELY IT IS A FAMILAR STORY-- HOW DOES ONE AVOID BEING SENT TO A VERY NICE LOOKING NURSING HOME WHERE THEY WILL GIVE YOU PILLS AND SIT YOU IN THE CORNER TIL YOU FALL OVER???—

I CERTAINLY DON'T WANT TO GO THERE! MY SOLUTION IS TO INVITE ALL SORTS OF STRANGERS INTO MY HOUSE WITH THE HOPES THEY DON'T THROW ME OUT...

OCT 27 2017
ACCENTUATE THE POSITIVE- ELIMINATE THE NEGATIVE - LATCH ON TO THE AFFIRMATIVE (AN OLD SONG ABOUT NOT MESSING WITH MR. IN-BETWEEN.)
****

LIKE.....HERE WE GO.... I HAVE BEEN CARRYING LIFE SAVERS IN MY CAR- FOR MAYBE A YEAR NOW AND I HAVE FOUND #1. THEY HAVE TO BE IN A TIN BOX BECAUSE TEH SQUIRRELS LOVE THEM AND #2.. WHEN I STICK MY HAND OUT THE WINDOW TO OFFER A ROLL OF THEM TO A COP STANDING DIRECTING TRAFFIC, HE TAKES IT… AND IN MY REAR VIEW MIRROR HIS GRIM FACIAL EXPRESSION HAS TURNED TO SMILING #3
 EVERYONE IN THE CAR WITH ME HAS BEEN UPLIFTED AND IS SMILING TOO.
SOOOOOO.......THERE ARE PIECES TO THIS NEXT IDEA...---

THESE PEOPLE TO WHOM WE DONATE DOGS ... WE
ALWAYS TRY AND GIVE THEM TO PEOPLE WHO ARE...
OR COULD BE... OUT IN THE COMMUNITY SOMEHOW...-
IT IS A FACT THAT WALKING THRU A NURSING
HOME WITH ONE OF OUR DOGS, PAST TEH NURSING
STAFF (WHO ARE DEALING WITH DOWNERS SO MUCH
OF THE TIME,) CAUSES THEM TO LOOK UP AT THE
DOGS AND SMILE. IF .. NOT SAYING ANYTHING WE
JUST HANDED OUT A ROLL OF LIFE SAVERS IT WOULD
LIFT THAT ATMOSPHERE UP A NOTCH... PLUS... SO
MANY OF "OUR" RECIPIENTS ARE IN THE PROCESS OF
GETTING BACK INTO CIRCULATION-- CERTAINLY THE
DOGS HELP BY DIRECTING ATTENTION TO THE DOGS
AND NOT THE INFIRMITIES OF THE PERSON.   SO LETS
GO ONE STEP FURTHER... HOW ABOUT SUGGESTING
ANYONE WITH OUR DOGS GIVE AWAY AT LEAST 5
ROLLS OF LIFE SAVERS A MONTH... CARRY ONE IN
THOSE POUCHES ON THE HARNESS AND WHEN YOU
SEE SOMEONE DOING A DULL AND BORING JOB, JUST
HAND ONE OUT... AND DON'T EVEN SAY ANYTHING..
99.7% OF THE PEOPLE WILL LOVE IT... I SUPPOSE
THERE COULD BE 00.3% WHO MIGHT EXPLODE AND
CALL YOU #$%^&*&^%$# IDIOT...
BUT THAT IS NEVER A CHANCE NOT TO DO GOOD.
NOW TO ASK LIFESAVERS FOR A PALLET -- OR A
GRANT????

Adult Day Care & Nursing Homes

SDP creates random acts of kindness every chance it gets
and the Danes offer that same support naturally. This is one of
the many reasons that the Great Danes make exceptional
Service Dogs. They are calm, intuitive, attentive, intelligent,
and endearing, to name a few of the qualities everyone
appreciates. Carlene thinks people already know all these
things about her Danes, but I decided, as the author, to list

them all here, again, and brag about them, again. Until people really do understand…these dogs are life-changers.

Here's another great example. The following occurred at a Veteran's Event, where Finn, still in training, was representing SDP.

From the Doggie Daily—

November 19, 2016.
"Leaving the bathroom we came across a veteran in the hallway having a really difficult time after watching the show. He sat with his head in his hands trying to slow his breathing. Finn saw him and I told him it was okay and he walked right over to him and put his head in the guy's lap. Instantly calmed him and put a big smile on his face, a beautiful thing to watch. I called Finn and he pranced back over…"

Nursing Homes and Adult Day Care Centers. Somewhere around twice a week, or as often as the schedule allows, Carlene White and Judy Connors, often with a couple of Danes and perhaps a person or two in tow, visits nursing homes in her area. If you have ever had the experience of a nursing home, you don't need any imagination to see what a big deal this is. Simply put, there aren't very many interesting, fun, lively, warm and cuddly things going on in nursing homes. In fact, they can be downright grim.

These visits are my favorite thing that SDP does for the local community. My own father was debilitated by an awful disease and when we could no longer care for him at home, he moved into the local long term care facility. Let's just say that when animals showed up, it was a much better day than when they didn't.

For me, this is just another example of how Carlene may appear darn tough on the outside, but really, she's soft and thoughtful on the inside. Her father was a retired police officer (in her words, a "cop") and she was his caregiver, softly reminiscing that, even with Parkinson's, he had a Scotch at 5pm every day and never spilled a drop. It is so interesting what we remember and what we choose to forget. We all have different perspectives on aging, getting old. Being old. Carlene's daughter Janine puts it this way, "When I get old I don't want to be a vegetable; I'd rather be a fruit." I get the distinct impression she will never allow herself to be a resident in a nursing home.

From the Doggie Daily—

July 20, 2018
we went to (a nursing home in) Revere yesterday and as i sat in a wheelchair, just for somewhere to sit,....NEXT TO A 101 YEAR OLD WOMAN.... the pt guy came in aNd patted me in the head thinking i was one of teh residents... WHOA !!!!

These visits to local nursing homes resulted in progress even when she is NOT there. The SDP folks observed that while there are many televisions around the homes, they are rarely in use, or when they are, it's not interesting or educational. In a brainstorm moment, she decided get Explore.org on all the screens that she possibly could. And of course, she did. That is a very abbreviated version of that accomplishment! She is a force.

That is only one example of the support and involvement Explore.org (a purely philanthropic organization in California created by a gentleman named Charlie) has reaped upon SDP. The seven live cameras, such as the one that shows daily mail call, were donated and installed in 2012. SDP became its own channel, live 24/7/365, part of 'Dog Bless You' on the Explore.org website. The DD below explains, to some extent, how it all interconnects and results in the worldwide support experienced at SDP. I could not possibly omit this astonishing fundraiser: on Veteran's Day Weekend 2019 the folks at Explore.org challenged SDP and offered to match all donations over that four day period. SDP supporters pledged nearly $120,000 allowing us to reach, with the Explore.org match, the impressive Grand Total of $239,000. Enough said.

Actually, NOT QUITE ENOUGH SAID…Carlene decided to add this about the amazing Explore.org.
… IN A VERY ABREVIATED EXPLINATION… THERE IS CHARLIE- OUT THERE IN CALIFORNIA WHO IS OF THE OPINION ONE SHOULD NEVER STOP LEARNING. BEING AN AVID DOG LOVER HE STARTED DOG BLESS YOU, INTERNET CAMERAS AND WITH THE HUNDREDS OF LIVE NATURE CAMERAS ALL OVER THE WORLD AT NO CHARGE, WITH NO COMMERCIALS THESE LIVE VIDEOS ARE AVAILABLE TO ANYONE. YOU CAN WATCH BIRDS HATCH, BEARS CATCH FISH. PANDAS FALL OUT OF TREES AND GREAT DANE DOGS GROW AND PLAY AT SDP. SO A BUNCH OF PEOPLE BEGAN WATCHING OUR SHENANIGANS ANDTHEN SEND ME EMAILS AND COMMENTS… WE GOT TO KNOW A LOT OF THEM- THERE ARE ABOUT 1500 DAILY WATCHERS CALLED "CAMERA PEOPLE" WHO SUPPORT SDP IN AN ASSORTMENT OF WAYS.

From the Doggie Daily-

September 26, 2016
THIS (She is referring to the annual Dogfest, a celebration of all things SDP held each September) WAS AN EPISODE MADE POSSIBLE ONLY BECAUSE OF THE DONATIONS TO THE CHICKEN BRICKS... WHICH IS MADE POSSIBLE BY EXPLORE.ORG... DOG BLESS YOU AND CHARLIE OUT THERE IN CALIFORNIA.... ---- SEVERAL MADE REFERENCE TOTHE "SDP FAMILY" OF CP'S.. WHICH IT CERTAINLY RESEMBLES... (WITHOUT ANY FAMILY SQUABBLES) ONE SAID "DID I EVER THINK......? " NO... HOW COULD I EVER KNOW THAT THIS EXPLORE.ORG ORGANIZATION WOULD ENCOURAGE SO MUCH

PARTICIPATION WITHOUT ANY COMMERCIALISM...
SELLING ONLY THE EXPERIENCE OF EDUCATON AND
ENTERTAINMENT MINUS THE ADVERTIZEMENTS ABOUT
 BLOCKED DRAINS AND BUG KILLERS.
MANY PEOPLE ASKED HOW I GOT INVOLVED WITH DOG
BLESS YOU AND EXPLORE.ORG...
I HONESTLY DON'T KNOW.   .... AND ... I HAVEN'T HAD
TIME TO ASK.
■■■

September 8, 2019
Dear Carlene,
You have no idea how important your visits to nursing facilities
are. Due to crippling arthritis, I recently became a resident of
a long-term care facility. The high point of my stay here is a
weekly visit from a volunteer, a 77-year-old lady, and her
wonderful look-a-like Wanda pup. He makes my day when he
jumps up on my bed so I can give him scratches and hugs.
The weekly visit from this woman and her dog is the best
medicine in the world, and is what saves me from depression
and despair!!! …..
Keep visiting folks in care facilities. It's the most important
thing you are doing!!!
Laurel
well certainly one of them...
■■■

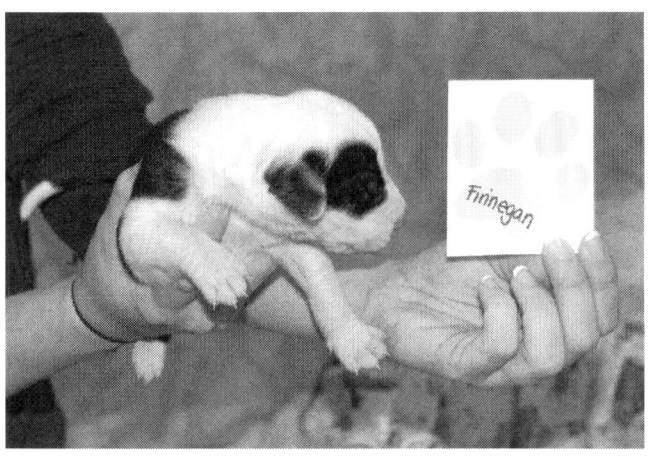

FINN AND EVE

Finn was partnered with Eve and went to his new home in Wisconsin from the Service Dog Project on January 6, 2017.

Eve's mother is wonderful enough to keep Carlene apprised of the progress and happenings, including fundraising, via email, many of which have been seen in the Doggie Daily.

When she heard about this book project, she reached out to me immediately with high praise and a great story which she was kind enough to share. The story, and Eve's poem, most of all, warms the heart and strengthens the soul. These dogs make people's lives better.

She wrote:
Honestly it can be so hard to find good enough words to truly encompass the impact Finn has had on Eve's (and our) life…..
I'll start with how we discovered SDP since that was all on me!
Eve has Osteogenesis Imperfecta aka Brittle Bones. At a young age it was clear Eve would have significant mobility challenges as she grew. I had always thought as she got older we would consider a Service Dog since we were dog lovers already & knowing it might help her to be more independent.

As Eve grew & her challenges became clear the picture of the traditional lab or retriever for mobility skills or retrieval skills didn't really seem to be a good fit. At this point she was still pretty young anyway & maybe not yet a candidate for many organizations. It remained in the back of my head but we were not actively seeking a SD.

Then one day on good old Facebook I ran across a video of Bella & George. It was after George (who by the way is Finn's brother from another litter - Finn's pretty proud of his big brother!) won the AKC Service Dog of the Year. I could see many similarities in the way Bella moved compared to the way Eve moved. Also I liked how Bella was able to hold on to George with her lower arm almost resting on George. You see walkers were often a challenge for Eve, she wanted to bend her arm at the elbow & lean on them in that position rather than holding on with her hands & using her lower arm strength which is poor. Bella seemed to be using more of her upper arm which would also be better for Eve! In that moment it was clear that this would be a great fit for Eve. I did a little more research online. I looked and looked for another provider of Great Dane mobility dogs. I didn't find one. I found where we could bring a Dane puppy to a trainer to have trained for a hefty fee. While willing to fundraise & figure out the money part I wasn't comfortable with the risk involved. It isn't until any dog works through training & matures that one knows if it is suitable as a Service Dog. That was not something I thought was worth the risk. I had learned that SDP allows the dog to choose the recipient, not the other way around. I believed this was truly the best practice. So after searching & searching for possible alternatives it was clear that SDP was the ONLY option despite the distance from the Midwest to Ipswich, MA.

SDP prefers to work with more local recipients, understandably & had only placed Danes with a handful of children. So I knew my effort at making this happen might not succeed but I had to give it a shot. We sent in an application & were given (what I call) a soft "NO". As a mother to a child with a rare disorder I have learned that I often have to advocate strongly to help others understand. Also I believed Eve was mature & intelligent enough for this responsibility, she needed it, really & not just for mobility. So I rallied our friends, doctors, physical therapists etc., they agreed with me & wrote letters to SDP & requested that they please reconsider.

After that Carlene reached out to me & helped to set up a meeting with another recipient's parent to share with us their experience. That was a great meeting it really gave us more insight about what to expect as well as the unique process at SDP. So, we decided to plan a time to take our family to volunteer at SDP. This would give us as a chance to really experience what they have to offer & to confirm whether this would be a good fit for Eve or not. In addition, Carlene could interview Eve & us in person. We knew this would likely be the first of at least a few trips to SDP to make this happen should we all agree it was in Eve's best interest. During that visit we cleaned kennels, folded laundry, stuffed kongs etc. & Carlene agreed to work with us but also warned she couldn't say how long it would take to find a match for Eve (she was 9), it often took longer with kids. So we tentatively planned a visit again for spring break. Well, Finn had other plans because the first time Eve went into his kennel Finn immediately warmed up to Eve & didn't run off like the others after she gave them cookies. Eve climbed into the upper portion of Finn's kennel & Finn followed right behind & hung out with her. I remember one of the "regular' volunteers, Maureen, passing by saying "oh Finn huh?" I wasn't sure what that meant but later in the day someone else said to me "I hear you're having a sleepover tonight - just something I thought I heard".

Sure enough we went back up to the house & were told Finn would stay in the guest house with us that night. We certainly did not expect that!!! Finn stayed in the guest house with us for the rest of our stay & through observation of the trainers it was decided that Finn had chosen EVE!! I was like whoa! wait! What??? It was just about week before Christmas so it was decided we would return in a couple weeks for training! So for us it went very quick much more quickly than anticipated & more quick than it seems for most. It was a whirlwind & to be honest a little overwhelming since it happened so fast. Service Dogs are amazing but in order to succeed as a pair & achieve synchronicity there is a lot of work involved, & training of the little person. For us since we were so far away it wasn't like we could just stop by & work on skills that we were challenging beside a trainer. I grew up with horses & was taught how to train my own so I was able to rely on that experience to help Eve learn to handle Finn & keep up his skills though the transition.

In Eve's words…
Carlene is an awesome person because of how many people she helps! & she's funny & nice to everyone but scary all at the same time!!

I remember one day we went to the store & was able to walk all the way into & out of the store. I had never done that before & I felt so proud of myself & knew I wouldn't have been able to do that without Finn.

We were at a cheer competition with my older sister. I was walking in the hall with the cheerleaders with Finn at my side. Suddenly the hall was filled with a sea of excited cheerleaders. I was trying to catch up with my sister's squad and was separated from my mom but it didn't matter because Finn was there & kept me from getting trampled. I wasn't even worried about it. If I didn't have Finn, I would have totally panicked looking for the safety with my mom.

I'm not walking a lot right now since I have had several fractures & surgeries in the past year or so but he's helping me get back on my feet. He helps me get into inaccessible place easier - like stairs. He also helps me keep up with my fiends on shorter distances.

Finn definitely also helps me sleep. My OCD used to keep me awake for long time but Finn helps me relax & I can fall asleep a lot faster with him in my room.

Finn is way cooler than a walker. I make friends pretty easily but Finn really adds to my popularity. Not only that but now when people stare at me they are looking at my cool dog instead of the "poor girl in the wheelchair" - Which I definitely do not need or want the pity!

back to Mom's words…
I would share some of the same stories as Eve especially like the one at the Cheer competition. In the moment I didn't think much of it. It wasn't until I caught up to Eve it hit me…. Like Whoa! I didn't totally freak out & worry that Eve might get knocked over & break a bone. I knew Finn would not only keep her upright but just his presence makes her "seen" so accidents don't happen. One time, before Finn, someone not seeing Eve knocked her over in a movie theatre & Eve broke her leg. So before Finn "the sea of excited cheerleaders" would have truly been a dangerous place for a kid with fragile bones. Finn just gives all of us more peace with Eve's safety, despite the fact that he weighs three times what Eve does. Not only that but he saves my back on many occasions by allowing us to forgo the wheelchair all together or saving me from carrying Eve up and down stair on a regular basis.

Finn is not your typical giant lap dog of a Great Dane. You might say he's a little aloof. But so very intuitive & definitely knows what/ who his job is! He always knows where Eve is & if he doesn't he must find her before he can do anything else. When Eve spends time in the hospital I take him out to do his business, we walk at the typical pace but when he is finished he can't get back to her room quick enough. If I could keep up he'd be running the halls back to her & seems to always know the way.
I find this such an interesting fact…. Eve weighs 50 lbs. & she is completely in charge of all of Finn's 155lbs!

And when prompted, Mom described the leader of SDP as follows, "Carlene is a riot. Set in her ways as she has earned it through all of her life experiences yet so caring, compassionate & selfless! I love her sense of humor & her non conformist whimsical ways!"

From the Doggie Daily—

January 10, 2017
Finn's 1st Day of School!!
Both Eve and Finn had a great day!
Despite the distraction of having Finn with her she still got her work plan done! Her teacher thought Eve may even have been more focused than she usually is!!!! She even wrote an amazing poem today which she gave me permission to share. Today is PAM day (infusion to make her bones stronger) she is not a fan of PAM day but the IV is in and meds are flowing. So Eve, me & ALL our furry friends are chilling on the couch!

July 3, 2017
Because of Finn, Eve has been able to do some walking for quite awhile in spite of the trouble she's been having in her legs! I am sure she would not have been walking at all if she didn't have Finn for the last couple months. It's amazing that he can help her stay strong and keep her upright for longer periods of time!!
We are so grateful for what Carlene does at SDP and all of the trainers, volunteers and of course the CPs and all who donate so that they can GIVE these dogs to the people who need them!
Eve had Finn have such a special bond and now, even though she isn't walking he is still assisting her. Together they are making nice progress in training Finn to help pull her wheelchair! Today we went all over Walmart with Eve in her chair and Finn at her side. They did it all without any help!!

July 15, 2017

FINN WAS PERFECT AT LUNCH AND ONCE AGAIN GAVE US THE OPPORTUNITY TO BRAG ABOUT SDP AND ALL FINN HAS DONE FOR EVE! OF COURSE THEY WERE ALL IMPRESSED!

BY THE WAY FINN BEHAVED AMAZINGLY PERFECT IN THE PET STORE EVEN WITH ALL THE GOODIES AND SQUEAKY TOYS. HE LITERALLY REFUSED ANYTHING IN THE STORE EVE TRIED TO SHOW HIM SQUEAKERS AND ALL!!!! SHE WANTED HIM TO PICK!! I HAD TO PUT A STOP TO THAT THOUGH BECAUSE IT'S ENCOURAGING THE EXACT OPPOSITE HE WAS TRAINED FOR! THIS DOG AND HIS TRAINING CONTINUES TO ASTONISH ME! WHEN WE GOT HOME HOWEVER HE DUG RIGHT IN THE TREAT EVE EVENTUALLY SETTLED ON. WE WERE ALSO SURE TO TREAT HIM AS SOON AS WE LEFT THE STORE FOR HIS OUTSTANDING PERFORMANCE!

December 12, 2017

FINN

The school that held the competition had many things going on that day so the halls were very busy. At one point, Eve and Finn (along with a few cheerleaders from Erin's squad) got separated from me and there were many cheerleaders between me and them. I knew approximately where they were and that they were with someone so was sure they would get to the right place BUT my eyes were not physically on her! I just realized this morning that in the past that would have sent me in to total panic mode! That is a scenario she could have very easily been knocked over and broken a bone or 2! She just isn't easily seen and she is not stable enough to stay on her feet alone if bumped. BUT she had Finn and I didn't panic at all. How can anyone miss Finn? And she has him to hold onto if bumped! What amazing freedom, independence, stability and safety the Service Dog Project and Finn has given to Eve but also to ME!!

These 2 are always reminding me of my gratitude to the Service Dog Project! What an amazing gift!

January 6, 2018
1 year ago TODAY we brought Finn home to Wisconsin from the Service Dog Project in Ipswich MA!
Wow what a journey it's been! I have to admit the first month or so I was a bit of a nervous nelly! (Which typically isn't my style). Eve received such an amazing gift of independence, freedom, security, companionship and BIG responsibility! But just as we were told it all came together in the timeline expected and Finn has become just a natural extension of her! He has brought so many new experiences to her life not to mention more mobility, strength and security! Clearly with the way he loves her she too has added much to his life as well. I just LOVE how when he looses track of her after running in the yard for a while or waking up from a nap the first thing he does is locate his girl! I could go on an on but I'll stop before this ends up to be pages long!
THANK YOU Carlene, the Service Dog project, Megan, all the volunteers & all of their supporters for an amazing 1st year! Looking forward to sharing many more to come!

November 15, 2018
Hi Carlene!!
Just wanted to drop you a note….
We just sent (via PayPal) the proceeds from the last Lemonade stand we did. Wow who would have thought a 10-year-old, a dog, a couple of friends & a lemonade stand would do that in just a handful of days! I'm so grateful that our home community gets to see, through Finn, all that you do for all of the recipients & that they supported them! I mean I'm sure you have many larger donations but since the initial goal was tripled in the end they are pretty excited about it!

I know it doesn't repay all you, your staff & the volunteers put into providing Finn to Eve but no matter what we raise it can't even come close to the value he has brought into Eve's life! She has had some down time but is back on the upswing & starting to be more mobile in the community again with Finn by her side! We brag about how amazing SDP is & all Finn does for Eve EVERY CHANCE WE GET!!

June 25, 2018
Eve passed level 3 of swim lessons on Saturday! Then…fearless SD Finn protected us from the ferocious creatures at the public library! … That stuffed ape really had him fooled and feeling like he posed as a REAL threat to our well being!!
Edited to add - Finn also got to brighten the day of several others waiting in the ER waiting room today we gave them our cards and told them all about SDP too!!
way to go!
****

May 6, 2019
....This right here encapsulates what Service Dog Project and Finn has done for Eve!! When we were at Discovery World. It's a large place and no way Eve could walk the whole thing at this point. So she was mostly in her chair. We came to this area... there were a few stairs, we stopped and her friends ran ahead for more hands on fun. Without Finn we would have taken several minutes to find a way without stairs or I would have picked up my 5th grader carried her down then carried the chair down. All options either cumbersome or time consuming and the moment may have passed. Instead Eve hopped right out and Finn was there to assist! She didn't miss anything or get embarrassed by needing my help! She was able to enjoy this area on her feet all because of Finn and everyone at SDP who shaped him into what he is and had faith in Eve's 40lbs of perseverance to be the handler of a (now) 160lb Great Dane!
We couldn't be more grateful!!

December 17, 2019
"to remind us why we do all this, another note from Finn and Eve."

Eve has not been receiving structured physical therapy for quite a while now…Well anyhow we felt it necessary to check in for an evaluation and consult. Her PT wanted to evaluate her walking with and without Finn and how long she could do each one before needing to take a break. Eve can walk more than 3 TIMES longer with Finn than without him!!! WHOA! Such an amazing priceless blessing! We can never thank Service Dog Project enough! I mean I knew he helped a lot but to put numbers like that to it was amazing!! Endurance is still a challenge but she said she was pain free. Just weak/sore muscles were the reason she needed a break.

Finn and Eve

COMMON SENSE

This sign appears in several very visible locations at the Service Dog Project.

"There is the tyranny of common sense," President Abraham Lincoln,1862, at the second annual meeting of Congress. "The dogmas of the quiet past are inadequate to the stormy present, the occasion is piled high with difficulty. And we must rise with the occasion. As our case is new, we must think anew and act anew. We must disenthrall ourselves (from the past and its experiences…) and not take the solutions for granted."

A hundred and fifty years ago our leadership realized that common sense was crucial to moving forward with new ideas and new solutions in this ever-evolving world. Innovation is hard because it makes people do things that are not easy or obvious. "A good idea is never easy to implement." --Carlene White, 2019. (She's probably been saying that for years…but not all the way back to Lincoln.)

From the Doggie Daily—

December 4, 2017

YESTERDAY'S SHATTING WENT BEAUTIFULLY,
...EVERYONE WAS DOING SOMETHING AND IT WENT
VERY WELL, CAUSING ME TO WONDER WHY I NEED TO
TRY AND MICROMANAGE THE STUFF THAT IS NOT
MICROMANAGEABLE. LIKE THE SIGN AT THE GATE SAYS,
"THIS IS A FARM, USE COMMON SENSE..." WHEN WE
KNOW FULL WELL SENSE IS NOT COMMON.
WE HAVE A FANTASTIC GROUP...MY EXAMPLE IS...HOW
MANY VOLUNTEERS HERE WOULD NOTICE A BOLT ON
THE DRIVEWAY AND STOP TO PICK IT UP—AND THEN
HAVE THE COMMON SENSE TO WONDER WHERE IT
CAME FROM AND TELL ME ABOUT IT (IT COULD BE THE
BOLD THAT WAS HOLDING THE TRACTOR TOGETHER....!)
5 YEARS AGO WE DID NOT HAVE MANY WHO COULD DO
THAT...NOW I BET 50% OF OUR VOLUNTEERS HAVE THAT
CAPABILITY...WHICH IS AN OUTSTANDING
IMPROVEMENT...

September 6, 2016

Carlene was describing a governmental certification process
and was quick to add (about the governmental member), SHE
WAS IN A TERRIBLE CRUNCH OF TRYING TO
LEGISTRATE COMMON SENSE.... BECAUSE IT IS NOT
ALL THAT COMMON...

A little more common sense from Carlene; "...maybe
cleanliness is next to godliness... but we should be able to
keep the place clean while concentrating on dogs... there are
times when I would like to see attention to the dogs and then
you can sweep the floor while they are napping. But it never
smells like dogs here, it smells clean."

Which leads to Poo Pickers. That's right, Poo Pickers. Unless
you have no imagination whatsoever you can conceive of how

much animal waste is produced by this many Great Danes, starting very young. Very young. In the main house, that beautiful cabin, which is where they are born and monitored 24/7 for the first few weeks of their lives. How is SDP able to achieve such cleanliness? Poo pickers. These small cardboard squares are the saving grace of raising a dozen or so puppies at any one time. Some of the employees are so good the picker goes where it should before the poo even hits the floor!

These little squares are an innovation of sorts, certainly. But the beautiful part is the second part; everyone who knows SDP wants to help SDP. So when Carlene has a request (a hat, a carrot slicer…to name just a couple, or stickers…) during her six-day-a-week 5pm mail call, she gets what she asks for, sometimes in more quantity than she actually requires. This is because everyone simply wants to help. Carlene got quite a few carrot slicers, perhaps even more than any working farm needs, so let me tell you that when she says she gets thousands of poo pickers, she means it. It all began when she mentioned that if you cannot afford a ten-dollar donation, (knowing that a lot of great folks cannot), send Poo Pickers. So, now, those CPs save up their cereal boxes and whatever else works, cut them up into three inch by six inch rectangles and mail them to Ipswich, Massachusetts. Literally by the thousands (and it's the ultimate in recycling!). After that mail call request years ago they had to find a storage area for all the packages. That's how many people pay attention to SDP. That's how much they want to help out. They are inspired, like the woman who met Carlene at some mall a decade ago. Inspired, even if she does not recall the encounter, they are still inspired.

In a complete and total moment of genius, one of the SDP folks took some of the pickers to a nursing home and had the residents decorate them. Everyone felt useful. And every little bit of help, well, helps.

Common sense in a nutshell:

CRAZY ACRES RULES
- *IF IT'S BROKEN, FIX IT*
- *IF IT'S DIRTY, CLEAN IT*
- *IF IT'S SMELLY, PICK IT UP*
- *IF IT'S EMPTY, FILL IT*
- *IF YOU TRIP OVER IT, MOVE IT*
- *IF IT'S GOT FOUR LEGS AND A TAIL, LOVE IT*
- *IF IT'S GOT TWO LEGS IN A GOLF CART, LISTEN CLOSELY TO IT*

GEORGE'S REPORT CARD

ARRIVES PROMPTLY

DRESSED APPROPRIATELY A

QUIET IN HALLWAYS A

RAISE PAW BEFORE SPEAKING A

PLAYS WELL AT RECESS A

FOLLOWS CLASSROOM RULES A

PROPER CAFETERIA BEHAVIOR A

SLEEPS DURING READING A+

SLEEPS DURING WRITING A+

SLEEPS DURING SPELLING A+

SLEEPS DURING SOCIAL STUDY A+

SLEEPS DURING MATH A+

SLEEPS DURING SCIENCE A+

PLAYS WITH OTHERS AT PE A+

COOPERATES WITH PARTNER A+

GEORGE IS A PLEASURE TO HAVE IN CLASS.

WE ARE VERY PLEASED WITH HIS WORK THIS TERM

GEORGE & BELLA

SDP produced George, who, in 2015, was awarded the AKC #1 Service Dog in the nation! Certainly something to be proud of. His person, forty-eight-pound teenager Bella, certainly is proud. Arguably the most recognizable team that has exposed SDP to the world, George and Bella are just as loveable as they are famous, paired together since George chose her, at age ten, on January 19, 2015.

George received the AKC's ACE Award, #1 Service Dog in the country, within a year of choosing Bella. She is now fifteen years old, weighs around a third of George's one hundred and fifty pounds, and has Morquio Syndrome.

According to Boston Children's Hospital, this syndrome is 'a progressive disease and rare genetic condition that affects a child's bones and spine, organs and other abilities.' Until she met George, Bella was bound to a wheelchair and crutches.

ABC News showcased George and Bella on November 4th of that same year and their world exploded, leading to a follow-up ABC presentation aired during the January 4, 2016 edition. That segment showed thirty-three Great Dane puppies in Ipswich Massachusetts, eighteen of whom were related to the wonderful George. What excellent national news for the New Year!
https://abcnews.go.com/WNT/video/young-girls-special-bond-service-dog-george-36089769

From the Doggie Daily—

December 18, 2015
BACK TO COMMENTING ON THE PERFECT DOG... GEORGE....I HAVE TO GIVE ALOT OF CREDIT FOR THE BURTON FAMILY.. RIGHT FROM THE "GO " THEY HANDLED HIM BEAUTIFULLY-- NOT MICROMANAGING. WITH TOO MANY COMMANDS.... BUT FIGURING THINGS OUT WHILE GEORGE DID TOO. WHEN THEY WALKED OUT ON THAT DOG SHOW FLOOR, GEORGE WAS CONFIDENCE ITSELF-
-" NO PROBLEM... WHERE ARE WE GOING?"
NOT TO MENTION BELLA TOO !! A NICE WAVE TO THE CROWD AT THE END-- PERFECT !
https://www.youtube.com/watch?v=KhUA2dLzho0&t=120s

WE ARE AT 67,300,000 AND COUNTING ON THAT FIRST ABC STORY...

Nine point one million people have watched this follow-up segment, from Inside Edition, dated March 10, 2016. It is entitled Dog's Best Day and definitely worth a few minutes of your time.
https://www.youtube.com/watch?v=Z9vSU1Yb_7A

April 26, 2016
THERE IS THE TV SHOW FROM JAPAN.... ABOUT
GEORGE AND BELLA--AND A TRANSLATION OF IT...
 THANKS TO A CP...(Camera Person)
 *If you have a few minutes, this is a joyous clip about the
Service Dog Project being shown on the other side of the
planet. Quite an accomplishment.*

Title: Bella and George
*Translated from a story on Japanese T.V. program…the
verbiage has it's own charm.*

*The narrator's introduction, "The story is about a girl named
Bella who cannot walk independently because of an illness."*

*The news clip itself, "In Boston, Mass., we visited a lady
whose name is Carlene White. She is raising a therapy
dog. She explains that therapy training starts three days after
a dog is born. In America, she raises Great Danes to be
therapy dogs. However, in Japan they train Golden Retrievers.
The reason is that in Japan, people are smaller in size. Great
Danes are large, approx. 80 centimeters high. Many
American's are tall and big. They usually need a larger dog for
assistance in standing up or walking. This story is about a
therapy dog who helps supports a girl in America.*

*This dogs name is George. He is 2½ years old. Bella is an
11year old girl. Bella is challenged by an illness. Bella used
to be very active. Then when she turned 9 years old, her
health started to change and the doctors told Bella's mom that
she has stopped growing. The doctors diagnosed Bella and
said she has Morukio "Shokogun" illness(?). Her kidneys did
not function properly and could not filter the good and bad
bacteria. This illness caused all the joints to stop growing and
she became unstable and weak. She could not play with other*

78

kids. Her body could not move smoothly. When Bella turned 6 years old, she became so unsteady that the doctors suggested Bella be confined to a wheel chair. She continued to endure surgeries on her neck, leg, and other parts of her body. She did not want to go out, because she could not play with her friends. However, she continued to do her treatments. She was able to do many things, but still could not walk. One day, she saw a handicapped person with a therapy dog. She found a woman who trained therapy dogs. It was there that she met George the dog. After she met George, she started to get a more positive attitude and believed she could someday walk again.

At first, it was difficult to walk with George. Bella started to walk with a crutch on the right hand side and on her left she held onto the dog. Also, going up to the steps, she would hold the railing with one hand and on the other side held onto George. After practicing with George, she was able to walk up the stairs with George without the crutch. She started to go to school. George stays with her throughout the day and she is able to play with her friends. She now smiles all the time. She can go any place with George. One day, Bella started to walk a few steps in the house without George's assistance. They sleep together in the same bed. Both George and Bella are happy to sleep together.

Then a miracle happened! She started walking in the snow by herself! Her dog George just watched her. When Bella's mom tried to get the dog to help, George pushed her mother away, as if to say, "Let Bella do it on her own". Also the dog tries to protect Bella. George not only supports her, he also is a good partner and playmate. Bella says "This dog is my best friend". She has been with George for 2 ½ years. He has also supported her spiritually. He has made her more joyful.
Watch it. https://youtu.be/219qDQjvKzY

Service Dogs aren't for everyone. They are a huge responsibility, they take care of us and we take care of them. What follows is an excerpt from the SDP website written by Bella's Mom. It can be found in the 'Inquiry' section designed to determine if a Service Dog is right for you and your family. It makes you think, as it was designed to do.

An excerpt from the website, and an expert on having a service dog in your home follows here--

WONDERFUL LESSON IN SERVICE DOGGING FROM BELLA'S MOM

So someone had asked about what we do for our service dog. You know we never had considered a service dog for Bella before seeing a mobility dog in action. It was a long year of us driving 30 minutes to Service Dog Project at least once a week to volunteer. Bella helped change waters, feed, brush, scoop poop, clean kennels, sweep, fluff fluffies and give pats with treats to many dogs over that year long period. The more you can be there helping out the better chance of a dog choosing you just like George chose Bella.

Is it always easy? Nope. It takes a lot of planning. With crutches there was no thinking involved. Bella could get up and dressed and then crutch to school or to a Dr. appointment. No worries. But when you add a service dog into the mix it takes more planning. "Bella did George go pee and poop this morning? Did George have breakfast? Do you have his vest/chain? Did he have 5 minutes to run? Do you have his coat if it's cold?" It's a lot to plan every time you leave the house. Then planning for the unexpected such as keeping a container in the car with water/ food bowls, treats, food, fluffies, and water. Does Bella always do 100% of his care? No of course not but she does 95+% of his care. She will happily take him to the bathroom, feed him, brush him, scoop his poop, and of course keep treats nearby.

Would we change anything? No way. Seeing the improvements have been amazing. Bella is so much stronger. But when you have a service dog you have to remember this is a 24/7/365 day job. Bella doesn't decide when she wants to use George or when she wants to use crutches. George doesn't stay home alone. He is always with us including overnights at the hospital. Has it changed anything? Of course it has. Are their places we don't go? Yup. Does it draw attention? Yes, at times Bella doesn't feel like saying Hi but she has to because she isn't allowed to be rude. So before you think of getting a service dog remember they require a lot of work, training, even after you think they are trained there is always more they need to learn, love, time and attention. Are crutches easier? Yup but we have adjusted our lives to include George and wouldn't change it for anything. It's not an option to give up on him and decide one day we don't want to put forth the extra effort. It is a lot of effort but he gave Bella her life back so we will do whatever we can to make him happy! But look at that face? What's not to love?
Love Bella and George

George and Bella receiving the Service Dog of the Year
Award
with Bella's Mom

FIFTY YEARS AGO

Carlene White is a mathematician by trade (an impressive list of International institutions contributed to the education) and was tracking satellites for the Smithsonian before most folks had ever even heard of satellites. And then, "I got married, and pregnant, and that was the end of that." She worked with a classified ad paper that delivered, her first task was one item delivered to wherever it should be in the back of a VW bug.

The company brought in this CPA to one of the meetings and he had a fancy printout, half an inch thick, you know the kind, with the stripes, all hooked together with little holes on each side to feed the paper. This must have been around forty years ago. Computers were new and most folks still didn't use them. Carlene had on a pair of overalls with a piece of paper in her back pocket that held all the information she needed to report at the meeting. No computer required.

He showed everyone his fancy computer results, and the other meeting attendees seemed impressed. "You are wrong," Carlene told him. Of course, he was surprised and asked how she could possibly know that. The wholesale price on the item in question was eighty-six cents. The total amount in dollars was an odd number. "That's how I know," she told him. She got the job of running that whole company, as it turns out. For three decades. By the end of her tenure they employed sixteen people and used tractor trailers, not VW bugs. She hardly ever went to the Main Office again…it just worked out better that way.

In 1999 Carlene was delivering packages, as hands-on as a manager can get, perhaps, in an impoverished neighborhood and came across a Great Dane tied with a cable. The kind of cable that recoils back when you loosen the tension. There were five or six kids there, teasing her, playing with her. It looked like she probably never got off the cable. Ever. The owner approached Carlene and they started discussing the animal. "I never should have gotten that dog," she told our hero, the Dane lover. "I don't want it." Certainly, and you can picture this if you know her even a little, Carlene did not hesitate. Even though she was working and already had a dog in the car, Rosie sure as hell wasn't staying in that situation. Turns out this beautiful Dane was in heat and Carlene had a stud with her. I'm sure that was an interesting ride home! So that's how The Service Dog Project, before it was even The Service Dog Project, got Rosie, who turned out to be a darn good mother, and a darn good dog, once given the opportunity. She produced two beautiful service dogs during her journey with SDP. She was never cabled again. Never.

She frequently reminisces about that position, "IT BECAME AVERY INTENSIVE ONE DAY A WEEK JOB LEAVING THE OTHER 6 FOR MORE INTERESTING THINGS.

BUT THERE WERE SOME INTERESTING MOMENTS...
I HAD TO GUARENTEE DELIVERY OF MAGAZINES IF AT ALL POSSIBLE EVERY TUESDAY. ONE FEB DURING A BLIZZARD, THE USUAL DELIVERY PERSON COULD NOT MAKE IT, SO I WENT OUT.. AND INTO A SMALL VARIETY STORE IN LOWELL MAS... IT WAS FULL OF KIDS- THERE WAS NO SCHOOL- THEY WERE ALL IN TH CORNER

STORE BUYING CANDY.. "I WANT THE PINK ONE WAY
BACK.. I'D LIKE THE 2 GREEN LOLLYS.." WHILE I STOOD
INLINE WHEN I FINALLY GOT TO HT E REGISTER I SAID
TO THE MAN..... " GEE YOU ARE AWFULLY NICE TO
THESE KIDS" AND THE REPLY....."WHY SHOULDN'T I BE...
MAYBE 1/2 OF THEM ARE MINE."

ANOTHER GOOD ONE..
IN LAWRENCE 5 PM .. MEN WERE PICKING UP TH
ENEWS AND CIGARETTES BEFOR HEQDINGHOME..M MI
WAS IN THE LINER.. I NOTICED THE MAN AT THE
REGISTER WAS QUITE MENTALY CHALLANGED AND
TEH CASH DRAWER HUNG OPEN-- PEOPLE WERE
REACHING IN AND TAKING CHANGE.. WHEN THE MAN
BHIND ME SPRANG FORWARD AND GRABBED A GUY
ASH EH HEADED OIUT THE DOOR... SLAMMING HIM
TOTH GROUND AND SAID " IN THIS STORE YOU TAKE
THE RIGHT CHANGE" . TRUE STORY... FOR THE REST
OF MY LIFE I HAVE BEEN CAREFUL.

ELVIS & FIONA

Elvis and Fiona were partnered in May of 2018 with tremendous, celebrated success.

From the Doggie Daily—
May 25, 2018
Well it has been an entire week since Elvis and I left SDP and what a week it has been!

We spent the weekend + Monday exploring campus and Boston as well as stopping for coffee with some fabulous friends! (Aileen and Jezlyn). Luckily Elvis loves going to Starbucks as much as I do. We also stopped by Northeastern University Police Department where Elvis made many friends and I want to thank them for all their support!

Tuesday was another hospital day and Elvis took everything in his stride. Everyone on the GI floor were so happy to meet him and extremely impressed as I walked down the hallway with no crutches! I have never been in Children's hospital without my crutches so you could say it was a little bit emotional when I walked through the doors without them! We then headed out to Cheesecake with Shea and Elvis was perfect. The waiters did not even realize he was there at first!

By Wednesday, Elvis had been exposed to multiple distractions including trains flying past us and children trying to jump over him but he has stayed right by my side. I then headed to my American Health Care class where Elvis was once again very well behaved (even answering some of the questions about Healthcare financing…)

Today was again another hospital day, which included Elvis meeting my primary doctor who was a big reason Elvis was a possibility! Elvis has decided he very much likes Dr. Fitzgerald! She also seemed less worried about me taking on the Boston Children's Hospital walk next month as I will have Elvis (it was looking like I would have to do it in a wheelchair before last week). Completing this walk has been a goal of mine for a while and unfortunately has not been a possibility in recent years so I am excited that it seems hopeful this year!

We also found out this week that the hospital is going ahead with another surgery. This surgery will be on my left leg as we are trying to prevent more damage and is currently scheduled for July 26th. We are still waiting for other surgery dates but for now we will be focusing on this one and the recovery. I think Elvis knew I was a little nervous about the fact I will be back in a wheelchair while relearning to walk so he made an extra special effort to cheer me up and reminding me that we are on this journey together.

So that is our update of the past week. It has gone by so fast and even though it has only been a week, Elvis has already helped me in so many ways, saving me from falls and helping me back off the floor. He has brought so many smiles to so many faces this week and I can't wait to see what our journey continues to bring! Stay tuned for more updates soon!
Love Fiona and Elvis

Sunday, September 9, 2018
ELVIS AND I HAVE SUCCESSFULLY MADE IT THROUGH
THE FIRST FEW DAYS OF THE FALL SEMESTER! THIS IS
ELVIS'S FIRST SEMESTER AND WE ARE DEFINITELY
BUSY. I AM EXTREMELY GRATEFUL TO HAVE
WONDERFUL PROFESSORS AND STUDENTS SO FAR
THAT HAVE BEEN VERY RESPECTFUL OF ELVIS. SOME
STUDENTS DID NOT EVEN NOTICE ELVIS WAS THERE
UNTIL EVERYONE GOT UP TO LEAVE

I MET WITH MY SURGEON AT THE END OF AUGUST AND
I AM CURRENTLY STILL IN A CAST AND WHEELCHAIR
BOUND. HOPEFULLY I WILL BE ABLE TO TRY SWITCHING
TO A BRACE DURING THE DAY AND A CAST AT NIGHT IN
A COUPLE WEEKS! ELVIS HAS FOUND THAT HE LOVES
TO PULL MY WHEELCHAIR, SOMETIMES I HAVE TO
REMIND HIM TO SLOW DOWN
 WE HAVE HAD A COUPLE ADVENTURES TO THE
PRUDENTIAL CENTRE AS WELL AS STOPPING BY J.P.
LICKS TO GET ELVIS SOME PUPPY ICE CREAM ON
FRIDAY EVENING AFTER BEING SUCH A PERFECT BOY
ALL WEEK   TODAY WE WENT TO WATCH SOME
HORSES AT THE BARN WHICH WAS A LOVELY BREAK
FROM CLASS, STUDYING AND THE HOSPITAL!

November 17, 2018
6 MONTHS WITH MY BEST FRIEND, MY OTHER HALF, MY
BUDDY AND THE ONE WHO KNOWS ME INSIDE OUT.
ELVIS HAS BEEN A BLESSING SINCE DAY 1, IT HASN'T
ALWAYS BEEN EASY, I PUT THIS DOG THROUGH SO
MANY CHALLENGES BUT EVERY DAY WE HAVE GROWN
STRONGER AND STRONGER. WE LEARN FROM OUR
MISTAKES AND MAKE THE MOST OF EVERY DAY. ELVIS
HAS CELEBRATED WITH ME IN MY HAPPIEST MOMENTS
BUT ALSO HELD ME IN MY WORST MOMENTS, HE HAS
THE BIGGEST PERSONALITY AND LETS EVERYONE
KNOW THAT HE IS INDEED... THE KING!

JUST OVER 2 MONTHS AFTER BEING MATCHED I HAD SURGERY ON MY ANKLE AND ELVIS IS THE REASON I WAS ABLE TO GET OUT OF BED TO TAKE A FEW STEPS SO SOON AFTER SURGERY, HE THEN SPENT THE NEXT 4 MONTHS PULLING MY WHEELCHAIR WHEREVER I ASKED, HE REMINDED ME ON THE DAYS I STARTED FEELING DEFEATED THAT THERE WAS A REASON TO KEEP PUSHING THROUGH. ELVIS HAS BEEN WITH ME THROUGH NUMEROUS HOSPITAL ADMISSIONS, PROCEDURES, MANY ER VISITS AND MORE HOSPITAL APPOINTMENTS THEN I CAN COUNT. HE TOOK ON COLLEGE LIFE LIKE A CHAMP, EXCELLING IN ALL CLASSES (ALTHOUGH HE IS NOT A FAN OF CHEMISTRY LAB!), HE GETS ME AROUND CAMPUS, AROUND THE HOSPITAL, AROUND BOSTON AND ANYWHERE I WANT TO GO. HE LETS ME KNOW WHEN I AM NOT FEELING WELL BEFORE I REALIZE AND MAKES SURE I LISTEN TO HIM. HE BRINGS A SMILE TO MY FACE BUT ALSO EVERYONE AROUND US!

ELVIS DEFINITELY PLAYS A HUGE ROLE IN HELPING ME AROUND THE HOSPITAL BUT HE ALSO PLAYS A BIGGER ROLE IN LETTING ME LIVE MY BEST LIFE, A LIFE LIVED TO THE FULLEST. WE HAVE FLOWN TO NORTH CAROLINA, WE HAVE GONE ON NATURE WALKS ON UNEVEN GROUND, WE HAVE GONE MINI-GOLFING, HE HAS PULLED ME AROUND BOSTON COMMON, WE HAVE GONE APPLE/PEACH/BLUEBERRY PICKING, TO RED SOX GAMES, QUINCY MARKET, THE SCIENCE MUSEUM, THE AQUARIUM, BOAT RIDES DOWN THE CHARLES RIVER, POLO GAMES, AND MORE. HONESTLY WE JUST TAKE ON EVERY ADVENTURE THROWN OUR WAY, WITH ELVIS I AM NOT AFRAID TO TRY NEW THINGS KNOWING I ALWAYS HAVE MY BUDDY WITH ME!

I AM SO LUCKY TO HAVE FAMILY/FRIENDS WHO LOVE AND LOOK AFTER ELVIS, I COULDN'T DO THIS ALONE AND I CERTAINLY DON'T. I AM ALSO SO GRATEFUL AND AMAZED AT THE SDP FAMILY THAT CAME ALONG WITH ELVIS. I FEEL LIKE WE HAVE THE BEST TEAM OF SUPPORTERS ALL THE TIME, THE MESSAGES ON

SOCIAL MEDIA, THE CARDS THAT HAVE BEEN SENT, THE COMMENTS PEOPLE MAKE TO US MEANS THE WORLD TO US. ELVIS AND I HAVE ALSO MET THE MOST INCREDIBLE SERVICE DOG TEAMS ON THIS JOURNEY WHO HAVE BECOME SOME OF MY DEAREST FRIENDS!

WE ARE EXCITED ABOUT THANKSGIVING BEFORE THE CHAOS OF FINALS THAT WILL FOLLOW. DECEMBER IS FULL OF FINALS, HOSPITAL APPOINTMENTS, PROCEDURES BUT ALSO CHRISTMAS AND MY BIRTHDAY (DESPITE THE FACT WE HAVE TO BE IN THE HOSPITAL THAT DAY!) I AM ALSO HOPING I GET INTO A TREATMENT PLAN AT THE HOSPITAL WHICH WILL HOPEFULLY GREATLY IMPROVE MY QUALITY OF LIFE. IT WILL BE 4 MONTHS BEING IN THE HOSPITAL AN EXTRA 2X A WEEK BUT I TRULY BELIEVE IT IS OUR BEST NEXT OPTION AND I KNOW I WILL HAVE ELVIS EVERY STEP OF THE WAY SO HOPEFULLY I WILL BE CLEARED TO START THIS.
I AM EXCITED TO SEE WHAT ADVENTURES OUR JOURNEY WILL CONTINUE TO TAKE US ON. ELVIS HAS CHANGED MY LIFE AS WELL AS EVERYONE AROUND US.
THANK YOU ELVIS FOR MAKING THESE PAST 6 MONTHS WITH A SERVICE DOG SOME OF THE BEST MONTHS NO MATTER THE CIRCUMSTANCES !

February 14, 2019
ELVIS AND I WERE ADMITTED TO THE HOSPITAL THIS PAST WEDNESDAY MEANING WE HAVE JUST FINISHED DAY 6 IN THE HOSPITAL. WE WILL BE HERE FOR A FEW MORE WEEKS. IT HAS DEFINITELY BEEN A ROLLERCOASTER THIS PAST WEEK! I DID NOT LEAVE MY ROOM AT ALL FOR THE FIRST 5 DAYS AND NOT VERY OFTEN SINCE THEN….
ELVIS HAS BEEN PHENOMENAL, I REALLY HAVE NO WORDS FOR HOW TRULY AMAZED I AM WITH HIM. TODAY WE FINALLY GOT OUT TO GO ON A COUPLE

SHORT WALKS AROUND THE HALLWAY AND WE
RECEIVED 4-5 DIFFERENT PEOPLE COMMENT ON HOW
COOL IT WAS THAT ELVIS WAS WALKING EXACTLY IN
STEP WITH ME WHEREVER WE WENT. WHILE ON MY
WALK I TOOK A STUMBLE WHICH ELVIS SAVED ME
FROM HITTING THE FLOOR AND AGAIN NURSES
COMMENTED ON HOW AWESOME HE WAS. WE HAVE
ALSO HAD MULTIPLE COMMENTS ON HOW CALM ELVIS
IS AND HOW HE JUST SLEEPS BY MY SIDE NO MATTER
HOW MANY PEOPLE ARE COMING IN AND OUT.
I TRULY DO NOT HAVE ANY WORDS TO DESCRIBE HOW
MUCH THIS DOG HAS HELPED ME EVEN IN THESE MORE
CHALLENGING TIMES. HE WAS LITERALLY FOOT
PERFECT OUT WORKING THIS AFTERNOON DESPITE
BEING STUCK IN THE HOSPITAL WITH ME. I WILL TRY TO
UPDATE A LITTLE MORE WHEN I AM FEELING SLIGHTLY
BETTER AS THERE ARE MANY MORE THINGS WE HAVE
BEEN UP TOO, MAKING SURE WE STAY OCCUPIED
WHILE IN HERE (ELVIS'S FAVORITE SO FAR HAS BEEN
WHEN BELLA AND GEORGE CAME TO VISIT!)

July 19, 2018
WELL WHAT A CRAZY PAST FEW DAYS WE HAVE HAD!
WITH SO MUCH GOING ON HEALTH WISE I HAVEN'T HAD
ANY TIME TO JUST TAKE A BREAK FROM THE
"HOSPITAL LIFE" BUT ON SATURDAY AFTER A HECTIC
WEEK IN THE HOSPITAL WE GOT ON A PLANE TO
NORTH CAROLINA!
ELVIS ACTED LIKE A COMPLETE PRO IN THE AIRPORT
AND ON THE PLANE! HE REMAINED FOCUSED
THROUGH EVERYTHING INCLUDING WHEN WE WERE
ASKED TO GO BACK AND FORTH THROUGH SECURITY
MULTIPLE TIMES. THE AIRLINE LOOKED AFTER US VERY
WELL, GIVING US PLENTY OF SPACE AND WERE VERY
ACCOMMODATING! ELVIS LOVED LOOKING OUT OF THE
WINDOW AND DESPITE GETTING VERY HOT IN THE
MIDDLE OF THE FLIGHT HE REMAINED AS COOL AS

COULD BE! IT WAS THE FIRST TIME IN A LONG TIME BEING ABLE TO WALK THROUGH THE AIRPORT INSTEAD OF BEING IN A WHEELCHAIR!

WHEN WE ARRIVED IN NORTH CAROLINA, ELVIS FINALLY MET MY DAD AND SISTERS! THEY INSTANTLY FELL IN LOVE WITH HIM…ELVIS AND I LAYED ON THE GRASS WATCHING EVERYONE PLAY AND JUST RELAXED. MY MUM ARRIVED MONDAY AND FINALLY THE FAMILY WAS COMPLETE! WE AREN'T ABLE TO GET TOGETHER MUCH AS WE ALL LIVE IN SEPERATE STATES/COUNTRIES SO THIS WAS THE FIRST TIME ANY OF THEM MET ELVIS!

…. I SMILED AND LAUGHED THE MOST I HAD IN THE PAST WEEK! ELVIS LOVES BOTH ALEX AND NATALIE AND CAN'T WAIT TO SEE THEM AGAIN! IT WAS VERY DIFFICULT SAYING GOODBYE TO THEM BUT WE ARE ALREADY PLANNING OUR NEXT ADVENTURE. ELVIS HAS LOOKED AFTER ME EVERY SECOND OF THIS TRIP ALLOWING ME TO DO THINGS I WAS NOT ABLE TO DO LAST TIME I WAS HERE AND IN THE TIMES I STRUGGLED OR MY HEALTH STARTED GETTING THE BEST OF ME HE PICKED ME RIGHT BACK UP! HE IS THE ONLY REASON I WAS ABLE TO MAKE IT DOWN TO NC FOR THIS SHORT GAP IN BETWEEN HOSPITAL DAYS TO SPEND TIME WITH MY FAMILY AGAIN!

ELVIS IS MY HERO！

TOMORROW IT WILL BE BACK TO THE HOSPITAL AND FIGHTING TO KEEP ME LIVING THE BEST QUALITY OF LIFE POSSIBLE! THANKFULLY I HAVE ELVIS BY MY SIDE TO MAKE SURE THIS HAPPENS.

LOVE FIONA AND ELVIS

August 27, 2019

"ENJOY THE GOOD MOMENTS. STAY POSITIVE IN THE BAD. KNOW THAT EVERYTHING WILL BE ALRIGHT."

6 MONTHS AGO I WAS IN THE OPERATING ROOM HAVING ONE OF MY ORGANS REMOVED…. IT'S BEEN A JOURNEY AND CONTINUES TO BE BUT I AM SO PROUD

OF LIFE I HAVE BEEN ABLE TO LIVE THESE PAST 6 MONTHS. THE OPPORTUNITIES I HAVE BEEN GIVEN, THE PEOPLE I HAVE MET AND THE GOALS I ACHIEVE MAKE THESE TOUGH MOMENTS WORTH IT.

TODAY I WAS ALSO INFORMED THAT I HAVE BEEN AWARDED THE RALPH AND THERESA ANSELMO RESILIENCE AWARD GIVEN TO A NORTHEASTERN STUDENT WHO SHOWS RESILIENCE AND PERSEVERANCE.

SO ELVIS AND I WILL CONTINUE TO LIVE LIFE TO FULLEST AND APPRECIATE THE GOOD MOMENTS, AND WORK THROUGH THE NOT SO GOOD, WHILE WE CONTINUE ON THIS CRAZY JOURNEY! THANK YOU TO EVERYONE WHO HAS BEEN APART OF THE PAST 6 MONTHS!

••

September 3, 2019

WELL ELVIS SURPRISES ME EVERY DAY... HE PUTS UP WITH SO MUCH AND TAKES EVERYTHING IN HIS STRIDE. THIS PAST WEEK WE WENT TO A PATRIOTS PRE-SEASON GAME AND ELVIS WAS A PRO NAVIGATING THE CROWDS AND LAID BY OUR FEET THROUGH THE ENTIRE GAME DESPITE THE NOISE. THEN HE WAS REALLY PUT TO THE TEST WHEN WE WENT TO A CONCERT LAST NIGHT. WE HAD GOT SEATS TOWARDS THE BACK OF FENWAY BUT AFTER A MIX UP WITH THEM NOT BEING ACCESSIBLE SEATS WE WERE MOVED TO THE VERY FRONT! AT FIRST I WAS A LITTLE CONCERNED THAT BEING THIS CLOSE TO THE FRONT WAS GOING TO BE TOUGH DUE TO THE NOISE, VIBRATIONS AND FLASHING LIGHTS. I WENT WITH MY CLOSE FRIEND SHEA AND WE BOTH SAID THAT IF AT ANY POINT ELVIS SEEMED UNCOMFORTABLE AND WANTED TO LEAVE WE WOULD WITHOUT HESITATION. THE CONCERT STARTED AND ELVIS LAID BY OUR FEET FOR THE ENTIRE CONCERT, OCCASIONALLY LOOKING UP TO SEE WHAT WAS HAPPENING BUT OTHERWISE JUST LAID WRAPPED IN HIS FLUFFY. HE THEN CALMLY

NAVIGATED ME THROUGH THE CROWDS ON THE WAY OUT OF FENWAY AT THE END. WE VERY ALMOST GOT TRAMPLED BY A CROWD RUNNING TOWARDS THE STAGE BUT ELVIS JUST REMAINED BY MY SIDE WITHOUT MISSING A STEP. WE ALSO PASSED MULTIPLE POLICE DOGS AT BOTH VENUES AND IT WAS NICE TO WATCH BOTH DOGS WALK PAST WITHOUT ANY HESITATION, STOPPING, OR ACKNOWLEDGEMENT. THESE ARE TWO THINGS I WOULD NEVER HAVE GONE TO BEFORE ELVIS AND I HONESTLY HAVE NO WORDS FOR HOW INCREDIBLE ELVIS WAS THROUGHOUT BOTH EXPERIENCES. WE HAD MULTIPLE COMMENTS ABOUT HOW INCREDIBLY BEHAVED AND WELL TRAINED ELVIS IS. THANK YOU SDP FOR GIVING ME THE FREEDOM TO ENJOY THOSE GOOD MOMENTS WITH FRIENDS, TO CREATE MEMORIES I HOLD ONTO WHEN GOING THROUGH THE TOUGHER TIMES

*I HAVE ALSO TRIED MUTT MUFFS ON ELVIS AND HE HATES THEM. HE IS MUCH HAPPIER WITH NOTHING AND IF HE EVER SHOWS SIGNS OF BEING UNCOMFORTABLE WITH THE NOISE LEVEL WE LEAVE.

Elvis and Fiona

SUNDAY STEW

Sunday Stew is the Crazy Acres' weekly Open House, truly open to everyone and anyone. You can bring something to eat (recommended!) or simply show up and pitch in. What a stew it is. There is always more than one project being tackled, always more than one conversation taking place, always more than one member of the public trying to learn, always more than one decision to made. Decisions that can ultimately affect lives.

A group of new visitors approached the table where Carlene and I were sitting and declared, "I met you years ago at the fair and was inspired." Inspired! An impressive statement, and a hell of a compliment! White takes it in stride. "People recognize me," she smiles and laughs, "I've been around." And then she tells me that she drove a team of eight miniature donkeys for years, tying antlers on the gentle beasts at Christmastime. She tells me about her neighborhood circus, how the animal training started, how it went on for years. The stories just keep coming, and more are created every day, even as I write this.

From the Doggie Daily—

October 14, 2018
i have this problem on a normal Sunday as i listen to someone explain to a new visitor some idea which is totally wrong...

there is a tendency for the public to figure out if you are here, you must know about dog training.... i listen as visitors ask very strange questions... i have to give linda teh gold star as she will quickly say "i don't have a clue" ---   so many othre people try and be helpful and answer the questions...too helpful can be a problem.

My first day ever at SDP was a Sunday Stew and the same day that the adult swing set became a reality, Labor Day Weekend 2019. I had driven six hours southeast from my home specifically to meet Carlene, stay in the beautiful log guest home that has housed so many successful dog-person pairings, and get the feel for the place. Three months prior she had contacted me about perhaps writing her story. She had read my first book and Scott Aubin's biography. I was intrigued; (how could I not be knowing Scott and Dash?) and so she put me on the calendar to stay for three nights. You have to write it, Scott had told me, adamantly. At least go and see the place! So I went. There is a feeling of peace and soulfulness. It's not surprising, in a place that helps so many people achieve independence and peace themselves. Everyone was very helpful, welcoming and sincere, intrigued at the prospect, I think, of a book about their leader.

Perhaps due to the Holiday weekend there were perhaps twenty folks working on projects for Sunday Stew. That is less than usually show up and therefore, we were all involved in everything. Since it was the first Sunday of the month, I was enlisted to assist in quite a tradition: Chicken Bricks.

The Service Dog Project exists thanks to the generosity of its donors and one of the primary fundraising activities is the monthly Chicken Brick board. For ten dollars each you purchase numbered 'bricks' posted on a virtual website wall. Bricks can be purchased right online via PayPal or by sending a check to SDP. They are sold out month after month, year after year.

The first Sunday of each month the numbers are printed on stickers and randomly placed on a slightly abused yellow vinyl tablecloth that has been sectioned off into squares (no small task, over twenty-two hundred numbers had been purchased for that day!). Three chickens are then released on the board. Once a chicken "shats", the owner of the number that is shat upon, or the number closest to the shat, gains membership into the 'Shat Upon Society of Ipswich' and receives a cash gift from SDP.

The chickens turn out to be very fast, hard to keep on the table, and also rather elusive with two of the three having no interest whatsoever in being caught and returned to their spacious enclosure. If you have not ever chased a hen with the intent of capturing it, the result is an incredibly laughable experience, as long as you can laugh at yourself. And if you are not laughing yourself, all the people that are watching you are definitely laughing! Those little birds can change direction on a dime and seem to sense where you may try to cut them off next! Anyway, one "shat" very quickly and after a considerable chase all were returned to the coop in good form. Chicken Bricks is definitely one of the most creative and successful fundraisers I have ever come across. Just writing this made me laugh at the memory.

The next morning, with a bent butter knife, I peel two thousand two hundred and fifty-three stickers (and the excrement that is required to finish the game) off of the chicken shatting board. It is a mindless task that allows me to set up this Mac on one corner of the cloth and type my impressions thus far in between sessions of bending over the low table. I am here as a Volunteer for the weekend as well as to have the opportunity to talk to everyone I run across.

It strikes me that even the chickens fulfill more than one purpose here; bug control, egg laying, protein production, and they work at the fundraising, too, to the tune of thousands of dollars a month (just enough to cover the payroll or thereabouts). When my task is completed, the cloth is carefully folded and stored on top of the refrigerator until next month. A brilliant, low overhead fundraiser, indeed.

See Chicken Bricks on the SDP website and then buy a few. I know you want to be part of it. www.ServiceDogProject.org

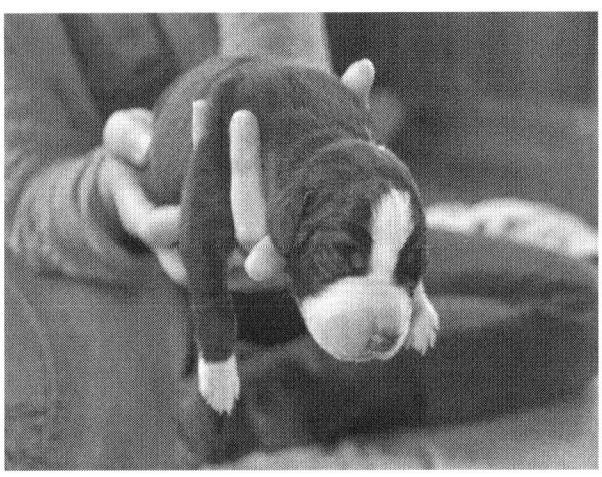

LUMI & HARRY

From the person (alias Lumi) via email. She and Harry were beautifully matched in April of 2013.

After my first visit (to the Service Dog Project) I was hooked. The people there were amazing and welcomed everyone like they had known them for ever.

I discovered SDP from their webpage and started watching the cameras then. I first visited for Sunday Stew shortly after that. My first memory is Megan (the head Dane educator) smiling at the guest house door welcoming people in. It was just a few weeks after discovering the project that I was paired with my Dane, Harry. Interestingly, he was the first dog that I ever met there.

The best educational part is when people understand how it works. I was working with large groups of children and they would say things like we know he is working and we pretend he is not here but we really like him. The Danes bring out the best in people, and they become captivated, just as I did. It tends to be the people that need the 'training,' not the dog.

Harry is very smart and quirky. Carlene says if you don't have a sense of humor then a Dane is not for you. They are 'velcro' dogs who love their person and always want to be touching their person or close by (perfect for a service animal).

They have no idea how big they are and will try to curl up on your lap. They let you know what they are thinking and what they want one way or another. Harry is very vocal and he loves being covered to sleep. When he gets up to turn and adjust when he is sleeping he will mumble until you wake up and cover him back under his blankie. They are giant baby love bugs and just want to be loved on and cared for and in exchange they will love you unconditionally.

I would love for people to know what this program has grown into and all the amazing people who are the cogs in this program that make it work. There is a lot of love that makes it what it is. Carlene started a program that has made amazing improvements in the lives of so many people. She has taken the unique aspects of the life she has led and turned it into this amazing loving community. She started something so much bigger than any one person involved.

From the Doggie Daily—

February 6, 2020
Hello
I wanted to send a quick note and some pictures of Harry. He is turning 8 next month. I can't believe how time has flown by. Every moment with this boy has been and continues to be a gift. I feel like we now so comfortably know each other that I can't remember what it was like before he came into my world. He is stunningly handsome and loves to play, run, and cuddle....

March 20, 2020
Hello Carlene!
Hope you are all well with all this chaos going on. I wanted to
send you an update for today, Harry's 8th birthday! He is a
happy lively and lovely boy. I never could have gotten here in
life without him. He is the most amazing piece of my whole
life. I treasure every second that we share together. It has
been an adventure and we have both learned so much from
each other. We challenged each other and I am thankful to
have the connection we have now where we just "get" each
other. 8 years ago a piece of my heart was born on boxford
road in Ipswich and I am forever grateful that he found his way
to me through sdp. He fills my life with love and joy every
moment.

As the final edit of this book came to pass, I contacted Lumi
and the other contributors to see if there was anything
additional to add. Here is her reply: "How can you thank
someone for a gift when that gift is so important that it
changes the essence of your being and improves your life
forever?"
I think, Lumi, that is a perfect way to say **Thank You**.

ORVILLE & SARAH

In Miss Sarah's own words, via email.
Orville and I have been together just over two years now, and this is our story...

"Each time I considered what to write for mine and Orville's SDP story, I tried to think of a spectacular instance that would make any one person simply say, "Wow!" or allow one to find some level of expected entertainment value in our experiences together. Over and again, I realized and reminded myself that our daily life tends to lack excitement, adventure, or entertainment value as depicted by today's societal standard(s). However, I also consistently remembered, and reminded myself, that Orville and I are fully content with our time together. I understand, in my own mind, that the excitement comes daily when Orville is consistently complimented on how he is the most well-behaved and well-trained Service Dog. The encouragement keeps us going.

Although our days, weeks, and months - soon leading up to our first full year together - repeat the same doctors, outpatient therapies, and surgical management procedures, everyone involved experiences visits with a completely different perspective. Orville brings relaxation for me, and my family, and an abundance of smiles to every office we visit. Everyone loves seeing him!

Having Orville accompany during all of our medical appointments has been a first experience for most all of our providers. Orville has had several "firsts" meeting the doctors, but thankfully, he has not yet encountered any new medical-related experiences out of our family "normal" - so that is always seen as something worth celebrating for all of us!

Besides his first experiences meeting new people, Orville and I have had other fun firsts together. The most memorable, thus far, was our first family vacation. Not only was it our first ever vacation together as a human family, but it was also Orville's first vacation and first flight! Though Orville wasn't always certain what to initially make of all the excitement, he had an awesome time at Epcot, met lots of new Disney friends whom adored him, and he was a tremendous help to me. I never would have been able to truly experience vacation without Orville's assistance. Being that he is so dedicated to his training, Orville offered me the encouragement and perseverance to keep up. I got to have much needed fun while keeping my muscles moving.

When first contemplating the idea of a mobility service dog, I initially couldn't grasp the concept of how mobility could be any easier with another moving, breathing companion capable of his own thoughts and actions. Now that I am experiencing life with a mobility service dog, it is difficult to imagine going back to my daily life without one. We don't need to live our lives for the excitement benefit of others. The "wow" is in the simple moments of our everyday that having Orville has made possible. Orville is truly the greatest addition within our family and the best buddy I could ask for. Here is to looking forward to more years of firsts and family fun."

Orville and I have since done other fun things together - such as going to the theatre for Cinderella, Singin' in the Rain, A Charlie Brown Christmas, and (upcoming this year) Rudolph. Orville enjoys himself a little culture every now and again. ;o) Orville has also started his second year "learning" piano with his youngest human sister, and attending Music Therapy - and outpatient PT, OT, and Speech - with his oldest human sister. He is quite the musically gifted pup! Orville has also learned some pretty graceful dance moves watching his sisters participate in dance.

Everywhere we go, Orville is asked to be an official mascot. I tell him that he will need a much bigger vest if he is ever awarded all of those honorary patches! Ha ha ha.

Orville reinforces all of Carlene's insight into what an excellent choice Great Danes are for Service Dogs, and how much they can surprise even those folks who already worship them….Sarah writes, *"This sounds a wee ridiculous when I have to admit it "out loud" on paper, but it has taken me almost the entirety of our current 2 1/2 years together to understand this portion of Orville's intuition and intellect. Orville always prefers to keep me within his direct line of sight, and he also indicates unrest of certain stranger's actions and personalities; however, there have been other repetitive behaviors that continued to keep me baffled. I could never understand why Orville insisted on laying by/in front of the exam room doors at the doctor's offices...especially after being bumped by them, time and again, each time they were opened for the providers to enter. In similar instances, I couldn't figure out why it seemed as if Orville would 'ignore' certain "come around, woah" commands to get him in a specific supportive position at my side. Instead, he would continue to come around my front, a bit further, and stop at an angled position. Despite numerous attempts each time, to correct his behavior, Orville insisted on conducting it his way.*
Well, I am happy (and slightly embarrassed, ha ha) to admit that I finally experienced the epiphany related to this behavior pattern. About a month or two ago, Orville and I were waiting at yet another doctor's appointment. I was seizing the opportunity to update our family schedule/agenda, and complete other paperwork, while Orville, again, insisted on laying in front of the CLOSED

exam room door. I proceeded to look up, and started to tell him he was being a ridiculous goof laying there, when it practically punched me in the face! Orville was laying in front of the door, as he had been for the last 2 1/2 years, not only to keep me in his direct line of sight, but also to "protect me" from the unknown on the other side. Since he was unable to see outside the door, he wanted to be certain that he knew what was coming through the door first, and that it was nothing harmful to me. Similar in the other instances, I realized why Orville would "come around" further than I had requested, and stand angled, while seemingly honed in on something 'random'. There is nothing random about his actions at all. In the other instances, I realized that my back was facing a door - with or without windows - and Orville would angle around the front of me so that he had the door, and anything behind it, in his line of sight.
What a sweet, protective boy he is! It is clear he has been extremely bonded to me, since an hour after we met, but I hadn't realized just how lovingly dedicated his big heart truly is. I am beyond grateful for him in so many ways."

When asked about Carlene, Sarah produced the following heart-felt commentary on the leader of SDP. *"I appreciate Carlene and it is clear that she appreciates all the Danes for their different personalities and abilities. She has perfected her craft, over several decades, but she also makes it known that she, herself, never stops learning from Danes each and every day. I view the majority of Carlene's personality as very direct and "matter of fact" when it comes to the Danes and all aspects of their care and training. However, as an SDP Partner/Handler, I find this/these encounter(s) informative and vital to the success of any Dane-to-Handler Partnership. It is necessary to appreciate your Dane for their individual personality and amazing ability, but it is crucial to remember that they are still dogs at heart - and, as the human, you have to remain the responsible one, LOL.*
No matter how brief, Orville and I have been blessed to have

other encounters with Carlene. She is truly an astounding woman, a wealth of knowledge, and she should be beyond proud of everything she has accomplished in her life. What an inspiration. It is our hope to see the work and blessings of Service Dog Project continue on indefinitely."
God Bless,
Sarah

CAN VS CAN'T

From the Doggie Daily—

October 4, 2017
DOWN WITH THE COULDN'T -- SHOULDN'T ...
WOULDN'T.. MENTALTY SO PERVASIVE IN OUR
EDUCATIONAL /LEGAL...SYSTEM.

I GOT SIDETRACKED-- IT ALL HAD TO DO WITH THE
CONCEPT OF   CAN   VS CAN'T
 AND THE WORDING OF THAT I N OUR APPLICATION S
 WE RECIEVE

ON OUR INQUIRY ---- THERE IS A "DO YOU WORK... DO
YOU DRIVE.... DO YOU VOLUNTEER?"
AND THOSE BECOME SIGNIFICANT ... NO ... YES...NO IS
NOT THE ANSWER WE ARE LOOKING FOR...
"NO, I CAN'T, I AM DISABLED..."
. COUPLED WITH " YES I CAN DRIVE... BUT DON'T
VOLUNTEER"   IS A MOST UPSETTING ANSWER
THERE MAY BE LOTS OF REASONS YOU DON'T WORK--
SOME OF WHICHI HEARTILY DISAPPROVE...
LIKE " I CAN'T WORK OR I WILL LOOSE MY DISABILITY

PAYMENTS..."

THAT IS SOOOOO MUCH DIFFERENT THAN
"I DON'T OFFICIALLY WORK-- BECAUSE I GET DISABILITY
PAYMENTS-- BUT I DO WORK AND GET PAID UNDER THE
TABLE FOR
A SIT DOWN JOB."
SOMEHOW, THAT ANSWER IS ACCEPTABLE TO ME...--
THE LEGAL MANEUVERS THAT MAKE IT ACCEPTABLE
ARE NOT
SOMETHING OF WHICH I APPROVE..
THE PERSON WHO LOOSES A LEG IN SOME
HORRENDOUS INDUSTRIAL ACCIDENT-- OR WAR....- WHO
TAKES A JOB AS A WALMART GREETER BECAUSE THEY
CAN NOT COPE WITH STAYING AT HOME-- HAS MY
ATTENTION.
*****

I REMEMBER... CHANNEL 4 IN BOSTON ... IS WBZ-- AND
THIER RECEPTIONIST WAS A GUY IN A WHEELCHAIR
WHO ANSWERED THE PHONE WITHTHE ONLY HAND HE
HAD THAT WAS USEABLE-- ANDHE WAS TERRIFFIC.. A
BRIGHT GUY-- I HOPE HE WAS PAID WELL...
I CAN NOT TELL YOU HOW MANY ARGUENTS I HAVE HAD
WITH DOCTORS ABOUT THE FACT THAT , YOU NEED
YOUR MOST ASTUTE, EDUCATED PERSON (?NURSE) TO
ANSWER THE PHONE AS A TRIAGE SITUATION...
INSTEAD OF THE HIGHHEELS AND LONG FINGERNAILS..
GREETER WHO IS GOING TO PUT THE PHONE ON HOLD
TIL THEY FIND THE NURSE ANYWAY.
***

HOW ABOUT A LAW THAT ANYONE "DISABLED OR
HANDICAPPED" WHO TAKES TEH JOB THAT REPLACES
THE "PLEASE HOLD" RECORDING MAY HAVE THAT JOB
TAX FREE IN ADDITION   TO THEIR DISABILITY.
PAYMENTS..
NOW THAT WOULD BE PROGRESS...

December 4, 2017
HERE IS A LIST OF WHAT I AM TRYING TO ORGANIZE--.. KE
DAILY !!! THANKS TO PAM'S EFFORTS OF ASSIGNING TASK
SOMEHOW........ WHILE I NEED TO BE ABLE TO ASK "WHO I
CHARGE OF FEEDING TODAY?"

BARN KENNEL MANAGER ROUTINE

? Any major health issues?

? Any heat issues?

pick poo

rotate dogs for quick run

organize morning volunteers

make bowls

change water

feed dogs

cookie off…

dog nap

water donkeys

hay donkeys

check post breakfast poo

Sweep

wash bowls

Restock

morning exercise run

rotate dogs

clean kennels

sniff fluffies

run washer

pick poo

organize afternoon volunteers

noon camera time

noon playtime lessons in arena

run dryer

check water

feed any lunches

cookie off…

fold laundry

repair todays broken whatever

hay donkeys

feed hens

collect eggs

water hens

chase loose hens

plug in tractor

pick poo

make bowls

change water

feed dogs

cookie off…

check heat   air condit

fill out who's where sheet

go home

(THAT IS A PARTIAL LIST)

THE UPPER MANAGERS DO ABOUIT THE
SAME MINUS CHICKEN CHASING BUT ADD
COFFEE POT FILLING.
KEEP STATUS QUO.
EVERYTHING ELSE.
FEED 8AM AND 4PM

THAT IS A PARTIAL LIST TO SOMEHOW FIT IN A
CALENDAR WITHOUT HAVING TO TYPE IT ALL EVERY
DAY??

112

March 9, 2017

it is kind of like the day they tried to kick me out of the mall with my service dog. i sat down and said " go ahead...call the police"-- and had great fun for 2 hours with security, and managers.

occasionally age has it's advantages....

actually... the rest of that story is..... pretty funny...

the manager and i sat for quite a while talking about service dogs and public access-- i wasn't moving... he finally said " i have seen dogs this big only once before-- when i was a manager in malden and they did a commercial" i said "stop there-- it was 2 spotted dogs with a schoolteacher looking woman with bagging stockings- and the dogs jumped up on the counter" he was shocked to hear it was me... with the bagging stockings - i was there with the dogs, and the actress they had lined up was terrified of the dogs... she was about my size so between makeup and stylist , i became a schoolteacher...

after that we became best friends and he stopped trying to throw me out.

that was liberty tree mall which we use all the time now. no more problems...
●●●

March 8, 2017

WE GET ALOT OF REQUESTS NOW-- THE WORD IS OUT-- THIS IS A FUN PLACE TO WORK... AND THEY WORK..----.SOME JOBS ARE BETTER THAN OTHERS.
THIS WHOLE CONCEPT OF COMMUNITY SERVUCE IS SUPPOSED TO BE A LEARNING EXPERIENCE.....
WELLLLLLL..... I HAD 4 KIDS WHO DID SOMETHING WRONG IN A CAR AND TEH JUDGE SET THEM TO 10 HOURS SERVICE... AND THEY HAD TO -- OR GO TO JAIL....SO I SET THEM TO MIXING MORE LIME IN THE MANURE PILE.. AFTER EXPLAING TO THEM THAT THE NAT'L HONOR SOCIETY KIDS GOT THE PUPPY MINDING JOBS . AND IF THEY THOUGHT THAT WAS UNFAIR "JUST WAIT TIL YOU HIT THE REAL WORLD."

MENDING FENCES IN BUG SEASON IS ANOTHER TRAINING
JOB FOR ONES REFERRED BY THE COURT.
IF THEY ARE ALREADY IN TROUBLE, I DON'T WANT TO GIVE
TEHM A JOB WHERE THEY COULD SCREW UP OR CAUSE
PROBLEMS... MIXING MANURE IS PERFECT-- CAN'T CAUSE
DAMAGE-- HERE'S A PICHFORK-- GO THERE.
ACTUALLY THERE IS ANOTHER 'I CAN'T STAND"-- A
MOTHER WHO CALLS AND BEGS ME TO HELP HER SON--
WHO JUST CAN'T GET HIS ACT TOGETHERE AND GOT IN
TROUBLE-- NEEDS CC HOURS-- SHE EVEN OFFERS TO COME
HELP HIM... NO... LET ME GUESS WHAT HIS PROBLEM IS...
LET ME PUT HIM IN THE MANURE PILE ALL BY HIS
LONESOME…

IT'S A GOOD THING NO ONE AROUND HERE SAYS "CAN'T"…

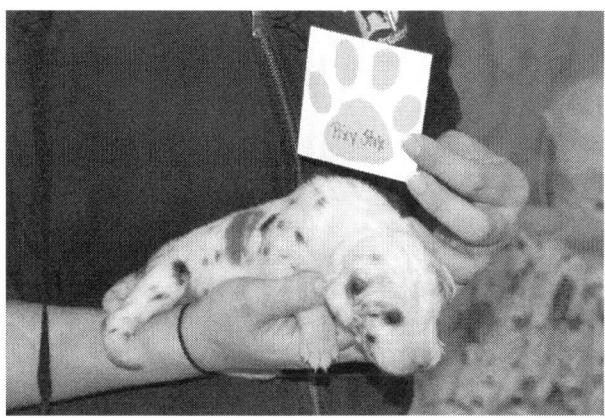

PIXIE & STACY

Pixie and Stacy were matched with an impact that is hard to measure on November 29, 2016.

From the Doggie Daily—

December 4, 2017
Good morning hope all is well. I just wanted to say this year has been absolutely amazing I am so grateful for what you and your staff have done for me by giving me Pixie to help me with my abilities to do all the things I lost out on. We have grown so much and with Pixie I have confidence, and conquered so many milestones. My heart is filled with so much gratitude for your kind act to help so many people just like me.
Thank you so very much I shed tears each day with how thankful I am.
I just wanted to send you a quick little thank you.

March 2, 2017
Pixie and I want to start off by thanking you for her new leads. When we revived them she sniffed away, like hmm these smell like some of my old friends have been near.

115

I have to say thank you again for your heart of gold again. Your devotion to help others is beyond words. I always tell everyone I meet all about how the SDP changed my life. I also want to thank all the amazing staff and volunteers that work so hard and endlessly to make such differences in people's lives like as in mine. Yesterday was 3 months when I first met my Sweet Pixie. She changed my life the day I met her. I knew we were destined to be together and we are now an inseparable pair. As I love to say I am 6 legs and 4 eyes. We are one! Sweet Pixie has in the 3 months helped me walk better which I never thought was possible. She has saved me from falls so no more broken bones. My feet really dislike stairs but Pixie is always on her A game. She has given strength, courage and so much confidence in myself. She is my HERO.

Pixie has not only changed my life but she my boys lives with all that they went through with having a sick mom. She has changed my youngest son fear of leaving me cause he knows that Pixie will be home or wherever I go off to protect me. As his teacher told me he stated one day to her. " I'm good now my mom is safe she has Pixie and she always helps her I can concentrate now." My oldest son is kinda on let me keep it all in. He will always smile and say hey I lost my job of doing something that Pixie has taken over.

She is truly loved and I'm blessed to have my sweet Pixie. Thank you so much for all you have done for me.

MARCH 14, 2017

Dear Carlene,

I just had to share this with you 'cause this is what shows how you have changed my life. Along with my youngest son who means the world to me. I always say I can never thank you enough for my life changing in the way it did and for all the endless work that the staff and volunteers do at SDP. Thank you so much for what you did not only for me but for my family and making my boys smile and my youngest learn to be braver then ever with all that endures with me. Pixie and Logan have become great friends to.

This is what melts my heart! Before my sweet Pixie I couldn't walk stairs without the help of my boys or family or friends and look at me go. Look at my boy smile in pride and pure happiness. This make me the happiest mom ever with all that he endures having a sick mom. Pixie is our Hero! Pixie is apart of me! We are one!

JULY 26, 2017

AT THE AQUARIUM --ALL THE STAFF AND EVERYONE THAT WAS THERE EXTREMELY CARING TO OUR NEEDS. THEY WHERE ALL IMPRESSED ON HOW PIXIE ENJOYED HERSELF AS MUCH AS WE DID. THIS IS WHAT MAKES ARE OUTINGS SO MUCH MORE EXCITING WHEN MY SWEET GIRL WORKS BUT ALSO GETS TO ENJOY HER DAY TO AT THE SAME TIME.

I HAD A LADY COME UP TO ME CAUSE HER DAUGHTER WORKED THERE AND HER DAUGHTER CALLED HER TO TELL HER A GREAT DANE SD WAS AT THE AQUARIUM SHE SAID SHE HAD TO GET THERE AND FIND ME, LOL. SHE SURE DID HUNT US DOWN. WE TALKED SHE KNEW JUST WHERE PIXIE CAME FROM SHE WAS SUCH A SWEET WOMAN WHO HAS A MOBILITY ISSUE AND I TOLD HER MY STORY AND NOT TO GIVE UP NOR TO EVER QUIT. SHE KNEW ALL ABOUT THE SDP WHICH MADE ME PROUD TO MEET SOMEONE IN MY STATE WHO FOLLOWS SUCH AN AMAZING PLACE.

PIXIE WAS A ROCKSTAR TODAY ON OUR FUN ADVENTURE I ALMOST TOOK TWO GOOD TRIPS 'CAUSE I JUST LOVE TO STUMBLE ON MY FEET. SHE SAVED ME FROM MY FALLS.

WHERE HOME NOW AND GOING TO ENJOY A NICE LAZY SUNDAY EVENING. I'M GETTING READY TO GO BACK ON CHEMO SO IT WAS SUCH A GREAT DAY TO HAVE NOTHING BUT SMILES ON MY SONS FACE, BEFORE I GET MY DOSE NEXT WEEK. THAT'S ALL THAT MATTERS TO ME IN LIFE. TIME TO START THE BATTLE AGAIN.

I HOPE YOU ALL ENJOYED YOUR WEEKEND AS MUCH
AS WE DID.

Pixie and Stacy

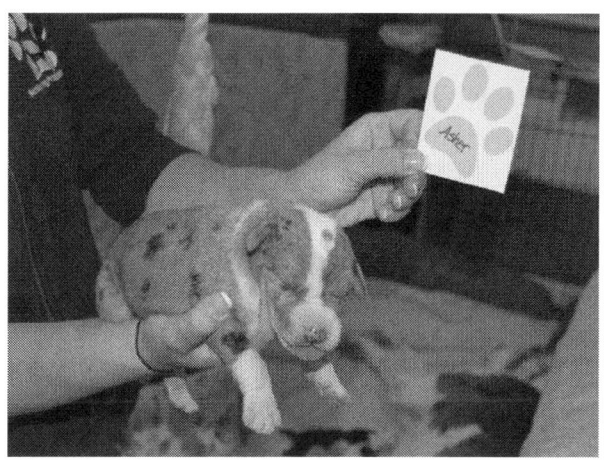

ASHER & ERICA

Asher and Erica were paired July 13, 2017 with life-changing results, for both of them. Erica tells her story on the inside cover of this year's SDP Fundraising calendar. *Just over two years ago, I was getting ready to embark on my law school journey, and though exciting, it brought up feelings of insecurity: my self-confidence vanished when I had to walk out to meet a client or walk into a courtroom. My gait was nothing new, but as I found myself in a field where exuding confidence was imperative, I felt so out of place.*

I met Asher in the summer of 2017, and my life changed. As people stopped looking at the way I walked to admire the handsome dog next to me, my self-confidence grew. …he takes everything in stride…in our second year of law school we accepted a summer internship disability rights law located in the heart of Manhattan. Asher's assistance has not only given me more mobility than ever before, but also the confidence to live how and where I want as I learn to be an advocate for others…I couldn't have a better partner to steady me through our grand adventure called life.

From the Doggie Daily—

WE'RE STILL PLUGGING AWAY AT THIS LAW SCHOOL THING AND WE'RE DOING WONDERFULLY AS EVER TOGETHER! IT'S AT THE POINT IN THE SEMESTER WHERE WE'VE JUST RECOVERED FROM MIDTERMS BUT WE'RE ALSO STUDYING FOR FINALS. WE HAVE JUST OVER A MONTH LEFT OF THE FALL SEMESTER – ALMOST DONE! POOR ASHER HAS BEEN SO PATIENT WITH ME AS WE SPEND MOST OF OUR WEEKENDS COOPED UP INSIDE WHILE I GET ALL THE READING, CLASSWORK, AND STUDYING DONE FOR THE BEGINNING OF THE WEEK. I'VE BEEN MAKING SURE HE STILL GETS PLAY TIME, OF COURSE, BUT I CAN TELL HE'S BORED COME SUNDAY AFTERNOON.
SO TODAY, WE TOOK A DAY OFF FROM HITTING THE BOOKS AND SPENT THE AFTERNOON IN DOWNTOWN PROVIDENCE, MY FAVORITE ESCAPE FROM BRISTOL AND SCHOOL WORK! IT'S HARD TO MAKE WEEKEND PLANS WITH FRIENDS BECAUSE WE ALL HAVE WORK TO DO ON OUR OWN SCHEDULES, SO I WAS ESPECIALLY GRATEFUL FOR ASHER'S COMPANY TODAY – IT'S ALWAYS MORE FUN TO NAVIGATE AROUND PROVIDENCE WITH A BUDDY, AND HE'S ALWAYS THE PERFECT GUIDE OVER THE UNEVEN SIDEWALKS AND STAIRS!
I'M SO AMAZED AT THE TEAM WE'VE BECOME IN ABOUT FOUR MONTHS. I WAS GOING DOWN THE MANY, MANY STAIRS IN THE PARK TODAY TO GET BACK TO THE BUS HUB, THINKING ABOUT HOW MUCH I ENJOY WANDERING AROUND BY MYSELF NOW BECAUSE I DON'T HAVE TO WORRY ABOUT NOT BEING ABLE TO GET AROUND SOMEWHERE OR GETTING WORN OUT ON A LONG WALK WITHOUT THE STAMINA TO KEEP GOING. I THOUGHT I WAS PRETTY INDEPENDENT BEFORE ASHER, BUT NOW I HAVE A BUDDY EVERYWHERE I GO TO KEEP ME COMPANY AND KEEP

ME SAFE ON OUR LONG WANDERINGS. I COULDN'T BE MORE THANKFUL FOR MY BEST FRIEND!

October 26, 2018
AND WE'RE OFF AGAIN – THIS TIME, TO WASHINGTON, DC!
OCTOBER HAS BEEN QUITE THE MONTH FOR US, WITH FOUR FLIGHTS AND TIME SPENT IN FAMILIAR AND NEW PLACES, AND I'M AGAIN SO GLAD I HAVE SUCH AN EASY-GOING, ENTHUSIASTIC TRAVEL BUDDY! TONIGHT WE HEADED TO THE DC AREA FOR TOMORROW AND SATURDAY'S EQUAL JUSTICE WORKS CONFERENCE AND CAREER FAIR. MANY OF YOU KNOW HOW MUCH I ENJOYED MY INTERNSHIP LAST SUMMER AT RHODE ISLAND LEGAL SERVICES, AND I'M CONTINUING TO EXPLORE OPPORTUNITIES IN PUBLIC INTEREST LAW. LAST MONTH I APPLIED FOR SEVERAL INTERVIEWS THAT WILL TAKE PLACE THIS WEEKEND WITH ORGANIZATIONS AROUND THE COUNTRY, AND I WAS TOTALLY TAKEN ABACK BY THE POSITIVE RESPONSE I RECEIVED. I TOLD MYSELF THAT THE TRIP HERE WOULD BE WORTHWHILE IF I WAS ABLE TO GET 3-4 INTERVIEWS OUT OF THE 15 POSITIONS I APPLIED FOR. I GUESS WE'LL BE STAYING BUSY, AS WE RECEIVED 12 INVITATIONS TO INTERVIEW FOR VARIOUS SUMMER INTERNSHIP POSITIONS!
WE'LL BE CHATTING WITH SEVERAL LEGAL SERVICES ORGANIZATIONS, AND THREE OF THOSE ARE SPECIFICALLY DISABILITY RIGHTS PUBLIC INTEREST LAW FIRMS AND ADVOCACY GROUPS. I HAVE SAID, LONG BEFORE I STARTED LAW SCHOOL, THAT I WANT TO WORK TO CHANGE LIVES OF PEOPLE WITH DISABILITIES AS MINE WAS BACK IN 2014. FACING DISABILITY DISCRIMINATION HEAD-ON IS SUCH A DEMEANING EXPERIENCE, AND I KNOW THAT I WOULDN'T HAVE THE KIND OF OPPORTUNITIES I HAVE TODAY IF A LAWYER DIDN'T STEP UP FOR ME WHEN HE

121

DID AND CHANGED THE DIRECTION OF MY COLLEGE CAREER. GETTING FIRSTHAND EXPERIENCE THIS SUMMER ASSISTING INDIVIDUALS DEALING WITH DISCRIMINATION AND ACCESSIBILITY ISSUES IS THE ULTIMATE SUMMER INTERNSHIP TO ME!

TOMORROW WILL BE A BIG DAY WITH INTERVIEWS FROM 9 AM TO AFTER 6 IN THE EVENING – I'M HOPING THAT WE CAN BOTH KEEP OUR ENERGY UP AND THAT ASHER DOES WHAT HE DOES BEST IN TENSE SITUATIONS: HE WINS EVERYBODY OVER! WE'LL HAVE A COUPLE MORE INTERVIEWS ON SATURDAY MORNING, AND THEN IT'LL BE TIME TO EXPLORE DC SINCE NEITHER OF US HAVE BEEN BEFORE! I THINK THIS WILL BE A WONDERFUL EXPERIENCE FOR US BOTH REGARDLESS OF THE RESULT, AND I WOULDN'T WANT ANYBODY ELSE RIGHT THERE WITH ME THROUGH IT ALL!

July 8, 2018

ASHER AND I HAD SUCH A FUN ADVENTURE YESTERDAY SPENDING THE DAY with the NEWEST MATCH, FIONA AND ELVIS--- ! THEY DON'T LIVE TOO FAR FROM US SO WE WERE SO EXCITED TO FINALLY MEET UP IN PERSON, AND ASHER LOVES ANY OPPORTUNITY TO MAKE A NEW FRIEND!

ASHER AND I HOPPED ON THE MBTA YESTERDAY MORNING AND HEADED TO BOSTON WHERE FIONA AND ELVIS MET US. ASHER HAD ONLY WORKED ALONGSIDE ANOTHER DOG WITH ME ONE OTHER TIME AND IT WAS JUST TO TAKE A SHORT WALK OUTSIDE, AND I WAS REALLY IMPRESSED HOW BOTH DOGS MAINTAINED THEIR FOCUS ON OUR WAY OVER TO CAMPUS. THE BOYS WERE INTRODUCED TO EACH OTHER OUT OF VEST INSIDE A QUIET HALLWAY OF FIONA'S RESIDENCE HALL – IT WAS SUCH A HOT AND HUMID MORNING, WE ALL PREFERRED TO STAY IN THE AIR CONDITIONING! BOTH ASHER AND ELVIS WERE A LITTLE BIT UNSURE AT FIRST ABOUT EACH OTHER, BUT THEY BECAME FAST

FRIENDS. ASHER, ALWAYS THE JEALOUS TYPE, DIDN'T LIKE IT MUCH WHEN I SAID HI TO ELVIS, BUT ELVIS IS SUCH A SWEET AND AFFECTIONATE PUP!

I'VE NEVER GOTTEN TO EXPERIENCE WALKING AROUND IN PUBLIC WITH ANOTHER WORKING DANE BEFORE, AND I'M SURE WE WERE A SIGHT TO BE SEEN WALKING AROUND DOWNTOWN BOSTON! PEOPLE WOULD STARE AS THEY USUALLY DO, AND THEN REALIZE THERE WASN'T JUST ONE HUGE DOG, BUT TWO! WE GOT THE USUAL QUESTIONS AND COMPLIMENTS, BUT PROBABLY MORE OF THEM AS WE PARADED DOWN THE BUSY STREETS! ASHER WAS THE SEASONED PROFESSIONAL HE ALWAYS IS, DESPITE HOW LITTLE TIME WE'VE SPENT IN BOSTON, AND ELVIS IS NOT FAR BEHIND! ASHER HAS OVER A YEAR AND A HALF OF EXPERIENCE ON ELVIS, BUT I WAS SO IMPRESSED WITH HOW LEVEL-HEADED ELVIS IS IN HIS YOUNG AGE AND LIVING IN SUCH A BIG CITY. NEITHER DOG EVER REACTED TO CONSTRUCTION, LOUD BUSES, OR THE OCCASIONAL FIREWORK YESTERDAY EVENING. BY THE TIME ELVIS IS ASHER'S AGE, HE JUST MIGHT BE A BOMB-PROOF DOG, TOO!

WE WENT TO GRAB SOME LUNCH IN THE AFTERNOON AND AGAIN GOT PLENTY OF LOOKS FROM THE CUSTOMERS AND STAFF AROUND US WHEN THEY NOTICED ONE DOG FIRST AND THEN SAW THE SECOND ON THE OTHER SIDE OF THE TABLE! FIONA AND I STAYED FOR SOME TIME, AND BOTH BOYS WERE CONTENT TO KEEP THEIR DOWN-STAYS AS LONG AS WE NEEDED, ASHER SNOOZED THE WHOLE TIME WHILE ELVIS WAS A LITTLE MORE INTERESTED IN HIS SURROUNDINGS – I'M SURE ASHER WAS WONDERING WHY THIS YOUNG PUP WAS WASTING SO MUCH ENERGY!

WE BEAT THE HEAT IN THE AFTERNOON BY BAKING SOME BLUEBERRY LEMON SCONES (WE THOUGHT WE'D INTRODUCE FIONA TO THE AMERICAN VERSION!), AND WE HAD TWO VERY EAGER FOUR-LEGGED SOUS CHEFS WHO WERE HAPPY TO MAKE SURE NOTHING

WAS DROPPED ON THE FLOOR FROM EITHER END OF THE COUNTER. THE EVENING BROUGHT IN A COOL BREEZE AND THE TEMPERATURE DROPPED INTO THE 60S, SO WE COULDN'T WAIT TO GET THE BOYS OUTSIDE TO PLAY! THEY COULDN'T WAIT EITHER AND HAD CLEARLY BEEN LONGING FOR THAT MOMENT THE WHOLE DAY. AS SOON AS WE WALKED TO SOME GRASS AND THE VESTS CAME OFF, THEY TOOK OFF TOGETHER AND WRESTLED AND JUMPED AROUND UNTIL THEY HAD WORN EACH OTHER OUT.

FIONA AND ELVIS WALKED ASHER AND I BACK TO THE STATION WHERE WE WAITED FOR OUR TRAIN BACK TO PROVIDENCE. ALL FOUR OF US HAD HAD A LONG DAY, BUT TIME FLEW! ASHER SLEPT ALMOST THE WHOLE TRAIN RIDE AND SLEPT LATE THIS MORNING – YESTERDAY WAS PROBABLY THE BIGGEST DAY EITHER OF US HAVE HAD IN WEEKS. WE HAD SUCH A GREAT TIME HANGING OUT WITH ANOTHER SDP TEAM THOUGH, THE LONG DAY WAS WELL WORTH IT! ASHER AND I ARE EXCITED TO WATCH FIONA AND ELVIS'S PARTNERSHIP CONTINUE TO GROW, AND WE ALREADY CAN'T WAIT FOR OUR NEXT TRIP TO BOSTON!

NOVEMBER 24, 2017

THIS THANKSGIVING, I DON'T EVEN HAVE THE WORDS TO SAY JUST HOW THANKFUL I AM TO HAVE ASHER IN MY LIFE, BUT I'LL TRY TO FIND THEM ANYWAY. HE'S A LIFE CHANGER: HE'S GIVEN ME THE ABILITY TO GO WHEREVER I WANT TO WITHOUT WORRYING ABOUT STAIRS THAT LACK HANDRAILS, UNEVEN TERRAIN, OR CROWDED SPACES. HE'S A BEST FRIEND: HE'S BY MY SIDE 24/7 AND IS THE BEST COMPANY FOR THOSE LONG NIGHTS OF STUDYING OR THE OCCASIONAL AFTERNOON NAVIGATING DOWNTOWN; EVERY DAY HAS ITS CHALLENGES, BUT I WAKE UP EVERY MORNING

EXCITED TO TACKLE THE DAY WITH MY BEST FRIEND BY MY SIDE. AND HE'S JUST AN ALL-AROUND SUPERSTAR: HE PUTS UP WITH LOUD AND BUMPY PUBLIC TRANSPORTATION, TRAIN RIDES, CONSTRUCTION, AND EARLY MORNINGS IN CIVIL PROCEDURE, AND HAS ALLOWED ME TO MEET ALL KINDS OF PEOPLE FROM ALL OVER THE COUNTRY. ASHER HAS MADE LIFE SO MUCH HAPPIER, AND HAS GIVEN ME MUCH MORE CONFIDENCE IN MYSELF ALONG THE WAY.

BUT, ABOVE ALL, I'M THANKFUL FOR THE PEOPLE BEHIND EVERY ONE OF OUR SUCCESSFUL OUTINGS AND I'M THANKFUL FOR THOSE CHEERING US ON. THE TRAINERS, STAFF, AND VOLUNTEERS OF SERVICE DOG PROJECT WORK TIRELESSLY TO CHANGE LIVES LIKE THEY HAVE WITH MINE, AND I'M SO FORTUNATE TO HAVE FOUND THEM AND BEEN PAIRED AS A RECIPIENT. ASHER AND I ARE ALSO SO THANKFUL TO HAVE BEEN WELCOMED INTO SUCH A LARGE COMMUNITY OF SDP SUPPORTERS – THE ARMY OF CPS WHO FOLLOW US ALONG AND MAKE OUR JOURNEY TOGETHER SO MUCH MORE FUN.

2017 HAS BEEN A BIG YEAR WITH LOTS TO BE THANKFUL FOR, BUT THOSE OTHER THINGS WILL NEVER QUITE COMPARE TO HOW THANKFUL I AM FOR MY DAILY ADVENTURES WITH ASHER.

••

July 6, 2019

HERE'S A FIRST: I'M OUTSIDE WITH ASHER SO HE CAN DO HIS NIGHTLY ROUTINE AND I TAKE HIM DOWN OUR USUAL BACK ROAD ON THE SIDE OF OUR BUILDING. MY BACK IS TO THE ROAD AND ALL OF A SUDDEN I HEAR THIS LOUD, BOOMING VOICE LIKE IT WAS COMING FROM THE SKY: "WE LOVE YOUR DOG." I TURNED AROUND TO SEE A POLICE CAR TWO LANES OVER AND THE TWO OFFICERS WAVED, ONE WITH THE LITTLE MICROPHONE TO THE EXTERNAL SPEAKERS IN HIS HAND. ASHER'S GETTING PRETTY WELL KNOWN AROUND THE NYPD!

Asher and Erica

SOCIAL MEDIA?

Constant Contact. I have heard Carlene talk about the mystery of computers but I am certain she is more adept than I am. The Doggie Daily, which you are now very familiar with, goes out to over twenty-five hundred email addresses every day. And over half of those recipients open the message and engage. It's an impressive number and an even more impressive percentage. Whenever I have sent an inquiry over the course of this research, the response can be almost immediate during the day and if after dinnertime the answer comes in before the sun rises, like this morning, at 5:41. In total she has sent out over three thousand of these daily updates; that's eight years of barely missing a day. Another impressive number. "Some things change, some things remain the same," she writes to me.

"I have a Facebook page?" Carlene asked me. "I'm sure you do," I replied, suddenly uncertain that if she didn't know...perhaps she didn't. Later that evening, during my stay, I decided to look it up. And oh yes, the Service Dog Project has a Facebook page. With 43,712 followers as of that minute. They gain another couple hundred each month, and by the number of 'likes' per photo, again, the engagement of the page is far higher than average, with six hundred or so folks weighing in on many of the photos and comments from matched pairs that you have read about here: George and Bella, Wendy and Gelato and Hunter, Dash and Scott.

The Facebook page topic is our first the next morning, and I tell her the thousands of 'followers' she has. "We do?" her eyebrows are raised. I am trying to decide if it's interesting or really she is much more concerned with what they are ordering from Purina. "You do, I sent you the link" I laughed. "Is that a lot?" She inquires and then adds, "What's a link?" Well, I think it's a lot, I have only a few hundred," I replied, laughing a little harder. We pull up the page and take a look. She laughs at me, and at the world of "social media." From her expression I can tell it's not her bag. Although at the same time she is often much more astute than she may let on…

During my research of the organization, I came across the following email, which describes her stance:

From the Doggie Daily—

August 27, 2019
let me get at least one thing strainght- i do not twit, link, face books, drop boxes...,or any other of the miriad of complications to sending a simple letter. i send this daily doggie out in bulk with constant contact- --CC-- only because aol would not send it out to teh number of emails on sdp list- there is some spam law- (tho from the #$%^&* i get,   i can't say the law is very effective.)

CC has some way of "unsubscribing" from the constant contact-- and they apparently do some checking for duplications... i don't.,, ocaSIONALLY ONE EMAIL GETS DROPPED AT RANDOM AND I/ OR YOU HAVE TO SWEAR YOU WANT TO RECIEVE IT .. STATISTICS??? OVER 1000 PEOPLE OPEN AND READ IT DAILY--- AND I CAN CALL UP EACH ONE BY EMAIL ADDRESS... AND I DO EVERY ONCE IN A WHILE -- LIKE WHEN I AM "ON HOLD" AND

CAN'T THINK OF ANYTHING ELSE TO DO. I HAVE A FEW
HIGHSCHOOL FRIENDS I KEEP TRACK OF BY SEEING
JUST WHEN THEY GET UP AND READ THE FOOL THING.

BACK TO LINKING AND TWITTING-- I DON'T EVEN KNOW
HOW TO ANSWER THE "INVATtions" i get in my emails--- i
am not ignoring you-- i just don't have a clue. and it is no
where near as important to me as keeping the dumpster
where the truck driver can reach it.
got to keep things in perspective.
■■■

Great Dane EPW (Extreme Puppy Watchers) is a Facebook
page that supports SDP but is not directly, officially,
connected. There are nearly thirty-one hundred followers on
that site, many of whom are also very engaged, and darn
enthusiastic about all things Great Dane. Follow them!

I NEVER KNEW

"I drove by here for eleven years before I stopped in," a local Veteran and Firefighter told me yesterday. He and his daughter had been here for hours, walking around, taking the tour, watching the chicken shatting, laughing, telling stories about military service and putting out fires, talking about life and the world. He crossed his hands in front of him and shook his head in pure wonder, reflecting my feelings about SDP. "I cannot believe this is here," he said softly.

He asked me why I'm hanging around and I told him. She is book-worthy his look tells me, this place is book-worthy. I have to agree. He concurs, it simply feels good here. Peaceful. We are standing in the visitor parking lot underneath old growth trees that move slightly in the evening breeze. I watch four Danes come tearing down the hill on our right and laugh to myself that when all these Danes get barking, it is probably far from peaceful…but it's peaceful right now. That doesn't just mean quiet, it means that it has a great feel. A presence. A soul.

I gave the Fireman a copy of *Knot Today* as he is a Veteran himself, involved in the local VA. He thinks, perhaps, that over the span of his retirement, he may want to take psychology courses. We talk about resilience. Resilience is a great word. We talk about Post Traumatic Stress and how it effects everyone differently, how everyone probably needs a different solution as the manifestation is so unique, unpredictable, hard to diagnose at times. So often it is hard to control the symptoms of such anxiety, I have seen that with Scott, and tell him about what a difference Dash makes in his daily life. We talk about how complex the brain is. We talk about other local facilities, there is a place called Rest Stop Ranch for assorted forms of dementia, we discuss the services for our Veterans, how hard they are to access at times. We talk about Critical Incident Stress Management, we talk and talk. At least half a dozen times he repeats himself— "for eleven years I have been driving by this place…" As I reluctantly pull myself away from the conversation, I hope that he keeps coming back to volunteer here, I hope that he gets involved. He would be an attribute for her, a good match for what they are doing here on Crazy Acres. Someone else who is interested in making people's lives better.

This morning I met a Volunteer named Bud (he can be a feature in the Doggie Dailies, I now realize, for his problem-solving skills.) I asked him the same question: what brings him here, a couple of times a week? "I'm reliving my childhood," he tells me, pulling an old photograph out of his chest pocket and offering it to me. I take it and peer down at an old fashioned black and white photo of a child with a Great Dane. "I had these dogs when I was a kid, and once I discovered this place twelve years ago, I was hooked. Every week I show up and do whatever needs to be done." He shrugs and helps himself to the buffet that is this Sunday's Stew. It's all delicious and home made and no one can resist Judy's carrot cake. Even I cannot resist it, and I don't eat sweets.

One of the service dog recipients answered my questionnaire with numerous comments about how SDP feels like a big family. And it does, even on my first day. There are three nests of Sparrows tucked in the top of one canvas shelter. It seems that no one here would imagine removing them, or even moving them. Everyone is welcome here. Another one of today's volunteers is wiping the Sparrow droppings off of the lawn mower seat before he can use it. Patiently, methodically, he does what needs to be done, as if parking under a bird's nest is something a 'normal' business would overlook. Poop happens, remember the sign at the main office? Pick it up and move on.

I ask him what brings him here to help out. He is a regularly scheduled volunteer. There is a long, thoughtful pause. "Something to do," he tells me, and I look sideways at him to see if this is the truth. It's part of the truth, I decide silently. He continues his story, pleased with my interest. "I drove past here, worked for the Environmental Department and checked things out right across the street at the lake, for twenty-eight years. Twenty-eight years," he repeats. "I never knew it was here. I saw the sign and drove right by." He has volunteered here for a year and a half or so, working on the landscaping, doing waste control, moving things around, driving the equipment. I talk to him about the feel of the place, the peace. They are doing something, (and he is helping), that improves people's lives with an ever-farther reaching web of interconnections and possibilities. Few people have that opportunity, or care that they do not.

PARTING SHOTS—

During my stay at SDP, conversations between Carlene and I dropped off and then picked up wherever we had left them, whenever we thought of something else we should discuss, another story that needed to be shared…it was an interesting, comfortable, peaceful, busy time, and I gained great respect for both her and her organization.

From the Doggie Daily—

January 17, 2015
Four score and seven years ago - i wanted to train service dogs-- now i am 100% successful and all i do is sit on this &^$$#&^* computer chair and swear at the printer, deal with "authorities" who tell me i must hang big red fire extinguisher signs next to red metal cylinders that could not possibly have any other use than to extinguish fires…

January 24, 2018
AMY CAME UP WITH THIS CLASSIC COMMENT ABOUT
SEAGRAM…
*"SHE ATTRACTS MUCH ATTENTION WHILE I AM JUST
SOME NONDESCRIPT PERSON ACCOMPANIED BY A
SKILLED, STUNNING DOG"*

November 9, 2017
ONE DISASTER AT A TIME IS DO-ABLE.

POOP HAPPENS.
PICK IT UP AND MOVE ON.

OCT 24 2018
If we ran an organization like henry ford we could put in one
end a piece of genetic material and 2 miles later out would
come a service dog.
The 1457 uniformed people would stand and put one piece in
place without talking AND LIFE WOUD BE SIMPLE.

September 17, 2017
SOMETIMES FOR THE BENEFIT OF THE ORGANIZATION
A WHIP HAS TO BE CRACKED...

September 9, 2019
These dogs don't just get you up the mundane curbs of life... it
is a whole new world (for the person)....these dogs may not
erase your disability but they certainly give you a whole new
ability.--- it has been said by several of our male recipients
that these Danes (even full grown) are as good as any puppy
at being a chick magnet.

February 9, 2015
SHOWING UP ON TIME IS THE FIRST PART OF DOING A
JOB. -- THAT WAS MY BIGGEST COMPLIMENT ABOUT
ANIMAL EPIOSODES -- I HEARD ONE DIRECTOR SAY
"WELL SHE WILL SHOW UP ON TIME WITH THE
CORRECT ANIMAL - AFTER THAT IT IS ANYONE 'S
GUESS"
••

January 27, 2020
there is a "just do it" element to this sdp operation.. take
betsy-- and her very fancy upscale gift ? store. i would
never suggest she take her 2-- (scarlot, mischa) and
have tem lie quietly in the corner of her store and greet
people going past them... but she just did it.
or the recipient who the first week after getting her dog--
-- took her brand new dog on 4 airplane flights teh first 2
days with absolutely no problem.
i do not have that kind of courage/.

i think the way it went was ... i told meg 10 years ago this
would work- and fortunately she didn't question my
advice and didn't realize i didn't know what i was talking
about-- before all of a sudden it was working./
if anyone offers you brains or luck... take luck every time/
••

July 14, 2014
THE REST OF MY COMICAL SUCCESS STORY-- I HAD
WORKED FOR THEM FOR 19 YEARS ALREADY WHEN I
MADE SOME COMMENT ABOUT BEING A MATH MAJOR
IN COLLEGE AND THIS PRESIDENT SAID "I DIDN'T KNOW
YOU WENT TO COLLEGE" WHICH SAYS A BUNCH OF
THINGS...

OCT 11 2014
AHHHHHH COFFEE...

PEOPLE CAN BE BOUGHT INTO RESPECTABILITY

An excerpt from one of my conversations with Carlene:
Work ethic used to include showing up on time. Somewhere I
heard there was a church that started charging the members
of its parish five dollars a minute if they were late for Sunday
Service. That inspired folks to be 'respectful' and show up on
time. Is that how we should become respectful? Be charged a
fee if we are not? I don't think so...

Camera Person Jennifer H sent this comment on farm
life..."Not a lifestyle for those who have to plan everything."

There was a truck delivering dog food (by the pallet) and the
driver was quietly refusing to back the truck down the hill to
the barn where the food is stored. One of the SDP regulars
said to that solid-looking young man, "If you can't do it there's

136

an eighty-year-old woman down there that can do it for you." The driver somehow found his abilities…

∎∎

"The dogs generally choose their person, it's not the other way around. The dogs know better than we do what works for them. They know what they need to do mainly by instinct, by the desire to assist, by the intuition this breed passes on from generation to generation."

∎∎

From the author. What I learned, sitting in Carlene's crowded, busy office on the last morning of my visit was how much I still had to learn. How much I didn't know. And there was a lot. And there still is a lot. Inquire about why a certain animal may be rejected as a service dog? Receive a color printout with photos and descriptions of proper gait and improper gait. Which is one of the differences between a potential service dog and a perfect pet. Questions about what's in the dog food? Receive a spreadsheet comparing the many ingredients in any pet food you can think of. Spreadsheet after spreadsheet. Fourteen pages in all.

As we watched the puppies eat breakfast in the office (which is also the entryway and the living room) I wondered out loud how the breed's colors occur, genetics or…? In return I was given another spreadsheet, this time with all the mated pairs listed on one side starting in 1994, some with names I recognized (Rosie, Bentley, Sizzle, Chaos) and going up through 2016. The spreadsheet is a lesson in recessive and dominant. While there are officially seven colors in the Great Dane, SDP concentrates on these four; Black (also known as Boston, generally with white markings), Harlequin (white coat, black markings), Merle (grey coat, generally black markings) and White (the whites can have splashes of color, but minimally).

Carlene has compiled this information and compared it to the Great Dane Club of America's percentages of coloration. Statistically, they are the same. Carlene White's attention to detail is proven once again. Her curiosity and passion occur in many areas that most people don't even wonder about.

What I have realized, after three days in her presence, is that the largest wealth of knowledge is Carlene White herself. We went for a quick breakfast and I took six pages of notes, jotting her stories and key words down. I hope that I have repeated them properly and mostly in context and understood their meaning. I hope I created a whole chapter on the topics she raised her eyebrows about, instead of emphasizing what she does not think is important. Sometimes the outsider point of view is crucial, sometimes it is not, and so I used my own judgment and tried to explain to the world how important this eclectic, energetic group of people is.

One of those dedicated people summed it up for all of us. "It feels good here. It's peaceful. There is a common goal. Assisting others. Making their lives better."

"This is character building," the volunteer coordinator tells me. "It's a happy place, a safe place for anyone who has lost a dog or a person or a friend or simply needs some peace. The dogs empower us to be better humans." Just showing up is therapy.

MORE DOG STORIES YOU WILL LOVE

From the Doggie Daily—

January 11, 2019
It has been three and a half years since Jess joined John. Jess has been a great help from the beginning, but even more so since as John gets older and his Muscular Dystrophy progresses the need for Jess has increased too. She has been up to the task. She anticipates John's needs in many ways. She helps him up from sitting, provides support while walking, adds the extra effort needed to go up an incline, and she also guides him around potential slippery areas when walking on snowy or icy surfaces and generally watches over him in all aspects of his movements. Everywhere they go people constantly comment on how well behaved she is, from busy restaurants to church to stores - Jess is always by his side. They have become known in many places in the local area.

Jess loves to help John unwrap his presents on birthdays and Christmas. She is always aware of who is going with the two of them in the car, and makes sure no one is left behind. We love to see how happy she is when she is working and are reminded how important it is for John and her to keep sharp, which they do. John does a fantastic job of taking care of her in every way. They are a great team.

We appreciate all the effort and sacrifice so many have made and continue to make so people like John can have a much richer life. Thank you so much for providing all the help needed to insure the success of John and Jess.

Happy New Year to everyone at SDP - workers, volunteers, and CP's!
John, Jess, & family
▪▪▪

SEPT 2 2019
TEH SWING SET IS UP! IT IS HUGE AND WILL BE A GREAT ATTRACTION FOR DOG FEST CHIP (the volunteer engineer) OUTDID HIMSELF-- HE IS TEH TYPE TO MEASURE THINGS WITHIN 1/16TH OF AN INCH-- WHEN WE PICKED UP TEH TOP PIECE OF PIPE BY TEH CENTER BOLT--- IT WAS JUST THAT ... THE CENTER.... AS IT BALANCED PERFECDTLY... I AM REALLY ITCHING TIO TRY IT,,, BUT I MUST WAIT TIL CHIP DECLARES IT READY FOR OPERATION...

CHIP ALSO REPORTS THAT HIS SON IS DOING A SUPER JOB WITH HIS NEW SERVICE DOG (ROO AND BEN)... MINUS TEH CRUTCHES HE HAS USED FOR YEARS, HE IS GOING UP AND DOWN STAIRS AND TEH DOG IS TOTALLY FOCUSED ON HIS PERSON, MUCH TO THE AMAZEMENT OF THE SCHOOL "AUTHORITIES"
▪▪▪

June 10, 2014
One of the CP's commented (when they saw me on camera) that I

seemed so calm and peaceful...how can you NOT be calm and peaceful when you're surrounded by warm, sleepy, or not, cuddly, feisty puppies for extended periods of time?

So, I'm grateful to you and to everyone at SDP, and to the CP's who supported me with their kind and funny comments...last week was one I'll never forget...I learned A LOT, my spirit was fed, and I will continue to spread the word about the miracles that are happening at SDP.

With love and hugs to all of you,

Clare

■■■

July 3, 2017

Hi Carlene,

Ava has brought smiles to so many, from the eastern seaboard to the Blue Ridge Mountains. At first people only saw only a beautiful dog with impeccable manners, but then they saw that she keeps me upright and their mouths dropped.

Ava made it possible to walk on the beach and to lighthouses, hike to a gorge in the mountains, and negotiate Washington DC. Poor Jim! Sometimes I had to remind him that he wasn't necessary, and that Ava did a better job.

Ava was a bit confused and nervous at first with so many new smells and people, but she settled into being a nomad and would "load up" quickly into her hammock bed with a cooling mat in "her" back seat. Both CPs and strangers were surprised by the change in her demeanor when the vest goes on and off; how calm and happy she is in work mode. And how she is a shy but friendly dog who loves to play without it. Thanks to Ava this was a great trip that we will always remember.

But a huge thank you to you, and everyone who helped to make Ava who she is! I was able to go places and see things that would not have been possible without her. She is such a blessing.

Cindy, Jim and especially Ava

■■■

December 12, 2017
SEAGRAM
LATELY, WE HAVE BEEN WORKING ON OUR FINAL FALL GARDENING TASKS TOGETHER. SHE DELIGHTS IN THE SUNLIGHT ON THE CRISP FALL DAYS AND ROMPS IN THE LEAVES WHILE I DO THE TASK AT HAND.

WELL, ONE DAY I WAS PLANTING A FEW FALL BULBS. SHE AIDED ME TO MY LITTLE GARDENING STOOL (IN VEST). AS USUAL, I THEN REMOVED HER VEST AND LET HER "GO FREE." ALSO AS USUAL, SHE CAME BACK TO CHECK ON ME A FEW TIMES AND I REASSURED HER THAT I WAS OK, SO SHE HAPPILY TROTTED OFF AGAIN. THEN I SLIPPED OFF MY GARDEN STOOL, FALLING BACKWARD SO THAT I WAS LYING FLAT ON MY BACK. I INSTINCTIVELY CRIED OUT AS I FELL, BECAUSE OF THE SURPRISE. FORTUNATELY, THE STOOL IS LOW TO THE GROUND, SO I DIDN'T FALL FAR AND WAS NOT HURT. ANYWAY, SEAGRAM IMMEDIATELY CAME BACK TO ME WHEN SHE HEARD THIS. SHE LOOKED ME OVER QUICKLY AND GAVE ME A COUPLE KISSES, WHICH IS VERY RARE, TO REASSURE ME. THEN SHE POSITIONED HERSELF TO HELP ME UP OFF THE GROUND WITHOUT ANY INSTRUCTION — ALL OF THIS WHILE SHE WAS OUT OF VEST. I GRASPED HER HARNESS AND WAS SOON UPRIGHT AGAIN.

WE ARE A TEAM, AND IT DOESN'T MATTER WHETHER OR NOT SHE IS FORMALLY "DRESSED" IN HER VEST — SINCE SHE IS ALWAYS READY TO HELP ME. SOMETIMES THE LITTLE THINGS REALLY ARE THE BIG THINGS. I AM SO GRATEFUL THAT SHE IS ALWAYS THERE TO WATCH OVER ME AND HELP ME. THIS HAS GIVEN ME THE FREEDOM TO RETURN TO SOME OF THE ACTIVITIES THAT I LOVE, WITH MORE CONFIDENCE. AND MY HUSBAND IS ALSO SO GRATEFUL, SINCE HE WORRIES

142

ABOUT ME FAR LESS WITH SEAGRAM AT MY SIDE. THIS IS JUST ANOTHER EXAMPLE AS TO HOW SHE IS MY SUPER SEAGRAM. THANK YOU FOR THIS WONDERFUL GIFT.

▪▪

October 14, 2019
Good morning, Carlene.
You are spot on...I didn't realize just how uncomfortable my upper body was using the forearm crutches until Bellow and I were matched. With Bellow, I am able to walk more in a natural position vs. the crutches which just helped me walk albeit out of proper alignment. A heartfelt thank you for your curiosity and drive to problem-solve, bringing your vision of SDP to fruition,
Cate & Bellow

▪▪

May 25, 2019
Dear Carlene,
I know I just wrote you with Rizz's two-month update, but I am so proud of her remarkable performance yesterday, that I want to share it with you.

We had a tornado watch while I was at work yesterday afternoon in DC at the Department of Agriculture building. When we get a tornado watch, we evacuate to the sub-basement of the building. As in all emergency situations, I have the option to shelter in place until emergency personnel can evacuate me. Seeing as how my office has windows and is on the top floor of the building, I decided it wasn't the best place to be waiting while watching for a tornado....I didn't want to be the first one to see it! So Rizz and I headed down the 12 flights of stairs with the hundreds of others making the same journey. There were people crowded in front of us and behind us, but Rizz kept pace with the crowd with, "step, brace, step brace, step brace...". When we got to the sub basement, the topic of conversation with everyone was how calm and well

behaved Rizz was. Since this was right at the time of the evening commute, when the tornado watch was over, we had to walk to the train station in a deluge of rain and stand in it on the platform while waiting for the delayed train. Also, since the trains had been delayed, the platform was packed with people and again, the topic of conversation around us was how good Rizz was. We ended the day by stopping at the store and while we were checking out, Rizz lay on the floor and rested her head on the bottom of the shopping cart and slept. It struck me then that this was just a 19 month old puppy that had a really hard work day! I know she will continue to mature into her work, but yesterday, she performed as if she had been doing this for years - thank you and the trainers for such a great partner!
Heidi

wasn't there a seeing eye dog who got her owner down 92 flights of stairs in the world trade center????

From the Author—Yes, there was, a Yellow Labrador Retriever named Roselle saved the life of Michael Hingson on 9/11/2001. Their story is told in a book called *Thunder Dog.*

June 10, 2014
Dear Carlene,
Today I went on a field trip with the 2nd grade classes to the Maine Wildlife Park and I brought Wendy on the trip with dad also. We saw a Bald eagle, a golden eagle, peregrine falcon, deer, moose, fisher cat, porcupine, skunk, all animals In the wild of Maine. Wendy did great and wasn't bothered by any of the animals.....except the smallest one if all.....the chipmunk! She is not a fan!
She helped climb a trail that said restricted from wheelchairs and stroller, and it would have been hard to do it with my walker but I had Wendy...my four wheel drive and didn't need to worry about!
The parents were asking where my walker was and I told them

I had Wendy now! Over roots and rocks, soft areas, up and down hills was easy peasy! The kids in my class did great and there were other schools there that did ask to pet her, but I said she was working and she could not not be petted. One kid asked why I was petting her and I said she's mine and helps me.

Some of the parents said they had to stay away because they wanted to pet her so bad, but they knew the rules because their kids told them. Wendy rode on the bus with me, right next to me. She liked to have her paws on me! Still need to work on getting on and especially off, the bus because the last step is so big....it is just hard for me. She passed this test and I did ok too!

We have been doing more at school and soon the summer will be here to be together all the time to get ready for fulltime at school in the fall.

Thanks for letting me have her to help and make things easier! We will be down for a visit soon!

Love, Hunter & Wendy

• •

October 25, 2019

Hi Carlene. Yesterday we had to go to upstate NY to take my mom for surgery. Well, her procedure was delayed, which meant we ended up being at the hospital for nine hours. I'm proud to say Bumble was his typical perfect self. He was so very amazing navigating through the crowds, staying when told to and calming my mom's nerves. Staff was amazed at how regal and smart he was as he achieved boredom and hung out all day. I handed out many of his business cards, which direct people to your website. A few people in the waiting room immediately went on the cameras and oohed and aahhed over Paula's puppies. My wife was telling a few very interested people about chicken bricks. We hope they buy some! Nine hours at the hospital surrounded by strangers was not hard at all for me but before Bumble is was impossible. Not only does he help me do everything physically but he really eases my fear of people. I could not

have survived yesterday without him. I would have had to just leave my mom and wife there and go hide at my mom's house. You have all changed my life. I can't thank you enough.
Scott C

February 20, 2019
Shauna and Kringle
Thank you for the gift of Kringle and beautiful life I am now having. You have changed my life.
The blessings of Service Dog Project are mixed. Kringle and the other dogs give the recipients the gift of mobility but you also get the gift of a new family. Yesterday not only did we have a lovely day with friends in Wisconsin but we got to meet a beautiful fifth grader, Eve with her dog Finn. My heart grew with how kind and happy this young lady was and her mother. I would never ask for my health issues but it is a mixed blessing because I meet wonderful people and experience great things. Thank you SDP and Eve's mom for making the magical meeting possible. It was a great afternoon. Eve is a lovely young girl who makes your heart grow! !
Kringle and Finn are brother and sister and tales were wagging.

Such a great day! Eve & Finn had a fun at Blended learning! Plus Eve has been trying to get some walking in more regularly! But the icing on the cake was the impromptu reunion of Finn and his sister Kringle!!!!!
How awesome is it that on their way to another destination Shauna and Kringle were stopping in the next town over from where we live!!! They even got to experience small town WI! They walked into a local establishment and their server was like "Hey I know a little girl with a Great Dane Service Dog!" Yep it was Eve and their server, a friend of ours! Annette Rude

146

Then this afternoon we got to get together with them!! And visit! ....so so glad we got together!
■■

November 5, 2017
Just wanted to share that Kringle and I completed our first 5K today. It will be 3 years on November 25th since my ruptured aneurysm so this was a goal for me. I never dreamed I'd be able to walk one again but I did, thanks to my girl, Kringle! Sometimes slow and steady does win race!
■■

Carlene even gets emails from the dogs themselves…and of course includes them in the Doggie Dailies…

Hewwo dewre Meesh Caween,
Dat gettun borned wuz a lotta wurk
Dat wuz one hek ub a tight hawlwayz. I awwmosht got shtuck!
Eef u nd Mama kuud jush git me headeeng in da wight diwekshun, I weowe twy to gitoawed ub dat fawzit.
Gotz eet!
Now eet duzn't take mush to feewl me up, shooo…I'z gunna need da napienap, nd den anuddewr, nd anuddewr.
Whut happeneded to da fawzit? Doez I hab to feewl my tum tum up outta Dat ting nowz?
Eet wuwrkz pwetty guud eef I howldz eet shteowe wit my footziez.
Dat fiwlded me up weawwy guud, shooo… I'z gunna take da nappienap, nd anuddewr nappienap.
Wowziez…! Me nd my buddiez iz fwee to wun up nd downz nd up nd downz.
Nd… maybee dwag fwuffiez wit ush upz nd downz.
Now wee getz to shtand up at da tabow nd hab owr bewwry own deesh ub pup pup keebow OR gwoowl. (chow)
Butz I shteowe need to git my wittowe napzienapz in cuz I wantz to gwow up beeg enuf to go in da box whewr… eef I sitz shteowe… dey woll da shenewry pashteded (mee) weawwy fasht!   I getz to meet wotz ub peepowez dis way.

147

I'z fouwnd dat eef I shtay bewwy kwosh to my own pwiibit pewrshun, dey find da wawrm pwacez in da cowld and da cowld pwacez when eet's too hotziez.

Nd da Foowd!! When dey fine shome, dey go nd hidez eet in da box dat's bewwy cowld to shneef. Nd moshtisist peekuuwiawr is… dey do da peez in da pewfewctwie guud watewr deesh.

Dis idea ub getting in da box sho dey can moob shtuff awoundz outshide da box is bewwy shtwange. Beww oftenz I geet out nd I'z shumwhewr ewlsh. Shumtimez when I getz out ub da box nd wook owt a weendow, shumone haz moobe da wuuwld way downz.

Shtwange tingz happen in dat wuuwld. I'z bewwy wucky to be abowz to nappienap in beetween da eppishodez. I met wotz ub peepowe my pewrshuun sheemz to wike. I wike mosht ub dem, but dewr awr onez owr twooz dat towrment mee nd shteek me wit peenz. I hab to gwin nd beawr eet cuz I woodn't wantz too upshet my pewrshun.

It'z gweat fun I get to go ebewwywhewr eshept fowr da stwange white woom dat shmewlz funny. Youz woodn't bewieve peepowe hab a speshow housh whewr dey awl howlz in unishun. I nebewr joinz in. My pewrshun duzzn't sheem to want me to do dat.

I am kawrefow to git many nappienapz in. I'z iz findeeng dat nappienapz awr mowr fun dan meeteeng da peepowe. Ish knot az fun to dwag da fwuffiez awound, I'd waadewr sweepiesweep on dem. My pewrshun finawwy notished I'd waadewr sweepiesweep dan wandewr wound so shee wetz me….

September 6, 2019
DEAR CARLENE,
THREE YEARS AGO TODAY, SEAGRAM WAS BROUGHT INTO THE GUEST HOUSE, WHERE I WAS ANXIOUSLY AWAITING THIS MEETING. IT IS HARD TO BELIEVE THAT 3 YEARS HAVE ALREADY PASSED SINCE OUR MATCH!

148

AT THE SAME TIME, SHE IS SUCH AN INTEGRAL PART OF MY LIFE AND KNOWS ME SO WELL THAT IT ALMOST SEEMS AS THOUGH WE HAVE BEEN TOGETHER FOREVER. SHE IS MY CONSTANT COMPANION, ALWAYS AT MY SIDE — EVEN MORESO THAN MY HUSBAND, WHO GOES TO WORK, WHEREAS US GIRLS ARE TOGETHER 24/7 (SHE SLEEPS NEXT TO ME, TOO).

SEAGRAM HAS BEEN SUCH A BLESSING, OF COURSE INCREASING MY INDEPENDENCE, AS WELL AS IMPROVING THINGS FOR MY HUSBAND, WHO CONFESSED THAT HE HAD BEEN CONCERNED ABOUT LEAVING FOR WORK BECAUSE HE NEVER KNEW WHEN I MIGHT FALL, AND IF I WOULD BADLY HURT MYSELF. HE SAID THIS SOON AFTER MY MATCH AND RECENTLY REITERATED HOW MUCH SHE HAS CHANGED OUR LIVES FOR THE BETTER.

THE BEST EXAMPLE OF HOW SEAGRAM HAS IMPROVED LIFE IS WITH STAIRS. STAIRS ARE SIMPLE ENOUGH, AN UNAVOIDABLE PART OF EVERYDAY LIFE THAT PEOPLE GIVE LITTLE THOUGHT — BUT FOR ME HAVE BEEN SUCH A CHALLENGE FOR YEARS. MUCH LIKE THE WOMAN YOU MENTION WHO WAS TRAPPED IN A PARKING LOT BECAUSE OF A CURB, I WAS SOMETIMES TRAPPED INSIDE MY HOUSE BECAUSE OF THE 3 STEPS AT THE FRONT DOOR. SURE, I COULD GET AROUND THE HOUSE WITH A WALKER — BUT THAT WAS NO HELP WITH STAIRS. AND IF MY HUSBAND HAPPENED TO TRAVEL FOR WORK, I WAS HOUSEBOUND FOR UP TO A WEEK AT A TIME, SINCE IT WASN'T SAFE FOR ME TO GET OUT ON MY OWN WITH ONLY A CANE DURING MY BAD SPELLS. BUT THAT HAS ALL CHANGED WITH SEAGRAM! STAIRS HAVE NOW BECOME AUTOMATIC FOR US, AND SEAGRAM MATCHES MY PACE SO WELL THAT SHE USUALLY NEEDS NO COMMANDS ON STEPS. IT IS INCREDIBLY EMPOWERING TO NOT GIVE STAIRS MUCH MORE CONSIDERATION THAN THE AVERAGE

PERSON!

AFTER WE VISITED THE FARM IN JUNE, AND ENJOYED SEEING & MEETING SO MANY PEOPLE & PUPPIES, WE WENT TO VERMONT BECAUSE MY HUSBAND HAD SOME WORK THERE. IT WAS A QUICK TRIP, BUT WE WERE ABLE TO FIT IN SOME FUN AS WELL. WE WENT ON THE TOUR AT BEN AND JERRIE'S — AND AT THE END OF THE TOUR, I FIELDED MORE QUESTIONS ABOUT SEAGRAM THAN THE TOUR GUIDES DID ABOUT THE ICE CREAM! ALL WERE SO IMPRESSED WITH HOW SHE HELPS ME! WE ALSO TOOK THE TIME TO APPRECIATE THE INCREDIBLE BEAUTY OF THE OUTDOORS IN VT. WE WENT TO A PARK, AND SEEING SEAGRAM AT MY SIDE, THE PARK RANGER RECOMMENDED A FLAT BOARDWALK. WE DID THAT, BUT IT WASN'T CHALLENGING ENOUGH, AND IT WAS A GOOD DAY FOR ME — SO WE FOUND A SHORT HIKING TRAIL AND GAVE IT A GO (MY FIRST ATTEMPT AT HIKING IN YEARS. OF COURSE THIS WASN'T LIKE THE HIKING I DID AT YOSEMITE MORE THAN 10 YEARS AGO, BUT I HAVE BEEN GETTING STRONGER WITH SEAGRAM AT MY SIDE, SO THAT THIS WAS EVEN FEASIBLE). IT JUST AMAZES ME THAT I HAVE BEEN ABLE TO GO FROM HOUSEBOUND TO HIKING, ALL BECAUSE OF SEAGRAM! (AND LOTS OF DETERMINATION ON MY PART HELPS, TOO)

THANK YOU SO MUCH FOR SEAGRAM!
AMY

September 23, 2019
Hello Carlene,
I am sure your weekend was full of thank you's from everyone attending Dog Fest, so I want to add mine. I wasn't able to attend dog fest, because I was attending my niece's wedding in Arizona. Going required a 5 hour flight and 2

hour drive after we had worked all day. The wedding was a typical cowboy wedding, held outdoors on very rough ground. As I played the wedding march on our Great, Great, Great Grandfather's 180 year old fiddle and watched my beautiful niece walk down the path to her future, I looked down at Rizz and was overwhelmed with gratitude for the sweet dog and all of the SDP community that made this moment possible. What Rizz gives me is precious moments.....Thank you and SDP for making this moment and all of our future moments possible!
Heidi and Rizz

September 22, 2019
I WANTED TO BE SURE YOU SAW THIS; FROM BUMBLE'S MOM:

NOW THAT WE ARE SAFELY HOME, I JUST WANTED TO BREAK DOWN WHAT LAST NIGHT'S MEET AND GREET MEANT TO US. OUR BEING ABLE TO BE THERE WAS SUCH AN HONOR. TO HAVE THE CHANCE TO ONCE AGAIN SEE SOME FRIENDS AND TO ACTUALLY MEET MANY OF YOU FOR THE FIRST TIME WAS INCREDIBLE. SO MUCH LOVE IN THAT ROOM! , HE (Scott, the person) DIDN'T KNOW WHAT TO EXPECT. HE IMMEDIATELY FELT AT EASE IN THE ROOM, SOAKED UP ALL THE LOVE BUMBLE GOT AND TRULY ENJOYED A SOCIAL OUTING FOR THE FIRST TIME IN OVER A DECADE. TO SEE HIM SMILE, LAUGH AND TAKE THE INITIATIVE TO ENGAGE IN CONVERSATIONS BLEW ME AWAY. HE SAID TO ME ON THE WAY HOME, "WE TRULY INHERITED AN ENTIRE FAMILY!" HE'S SPOT ON. AND IT COULDN'T BE A BETTER GROUP OF PEOPLE TO INHERIT. IT WAS A WHIRLWIND TRIP BUT I CAN HONESTLY SAY IT WAS THE BEST WE'VE FELT IN YEARS. THANK YOU ALL!!!

From the 2020 SDP calendar--

"Bumble's a miraculous game changer." Scott, Massachusetts

"Kringle and I have traveled with world and hiked while defying everything the doctors predicted. Words can't express the gratitude I have to SDP." Shauna, Pennsylvania

"Great Danes are simply the best for mobility work, I know I would be stuck in a wheelchair if it was not for this beautiful girl." Karen, New Mexico

"Stability can mean so much more than what you think." Dan, Kansas

"Because of Dash my spirit is unconquerable." Scott, New York

Our volunteers have been, in their previous existence –

Activity Director at a Convalescent Center

Applied Behavioral Analyst, Boston Public Schools, autism spectrum

Art Professor & Artist

Bakery Manager

Bowling, Senior League

Car Washer

Cartographer

Certified Vet Teacher

Civil Engineer

Coastal State Environmental Police Officer

Dartboard & Poker Chip Sales

Education

End User Computer Trainer

ER / Mental Health Tech

Exceptional Parent Magazine (for children with special needs)

Fast Food Worker

Field Hockey & Lacrosse Official, Youth thru College Levels

Finance & Administration Manager, Federal Reserve Bank of Boston

Frozen Food Sales

Gas Station Attendant

Graphic Designer

Hampshire College, Dual Major, Written Arts & Photography

Hypnotherapy

Information Systems/Technology Director at a school

IT Systems Analyst

Journalist

Licensed Clinical Psychologist

Licensed Mental Health Counselor

MA DPH Assistant Director, Drug Control Program

Medical Technologist and Hematology Supervisor

Mental Health Attendant

Minister

Musician

Newsgirl turned Academic Advisor

NOAA Fisheries, Regulation Development

Nurse Practitioner - Women's Health

Occupational Therapist

Office Manager

Old Time Photographers at a Carnival at Mike Bloomberg's house

Park Maintenance

Pharmacy Consultant

Photographer

Pizza Maker

Plastics Sales

Pool Cleaner

Professional Photographer

Publlshing

Registered Nurse First Assist

Registered Yoga Instructor

Restaurant General Manager

Restaurant Owner

Restaurant Worker

Sales & Marketing for Gillette

Salesperson of Video Streaming Platforms Military/DOD

Scrabble Club

Senior Technical Business Analyst

Teacher, College Level & K-12 Administration

Technical Trainer, Network Administrators

Tire Changer

UBER Driver

USMC

Venture Capital

Volunteer at Emmaus House

Worked on Nuclear Submarines

Worked with At Risk Teens Schools & Family Services

to be continued…

And a special note
TO WILLIAM HUBER AND MARK AMIRAULT
THANK YOU FOR THE PHOTOS!
You are so much appreciated for capturing the essence of these beautiful creatures so we can share them with the world…

MORE INFORMATION

Some of what follows is redundant with the content of the story, but it's important and perhaps bears repeating.

With volunteers and a minimum of paid staff, donations to Service Dog Project go directly to the care and training of their dogs.

Dog Bless You/Explore.org not only support us, but the seven cameras they maintain here have allowed a virtual community to develop. www.Explore.org

There are hundreds of "Camera people" from around the globe watch and donate which is a major source of our funding. We thank them sincerely.

The Tower of Hope's mission is to empower people who are living with a disability or a chronic illness to live more independently by providing these amazing animals to wounded Veterans. www.thetowerofhope.org

Purina, a Nestle company, donates our food… Purina Pro Plan - Savor Purina.com

**If you are interested in our organization or one of our
Superb Service Dogs,
please go to our website:**

ServiceDogProject.org

Thank you.

Service Dog Project

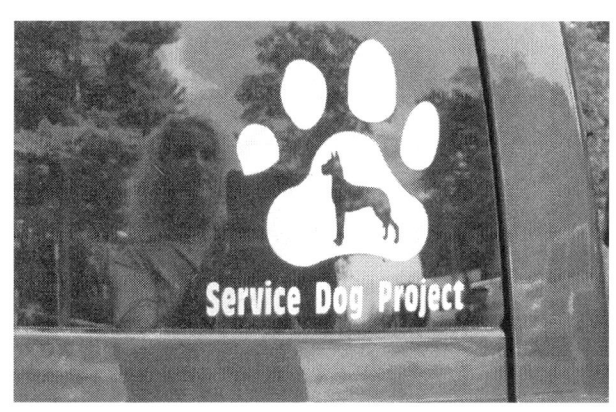

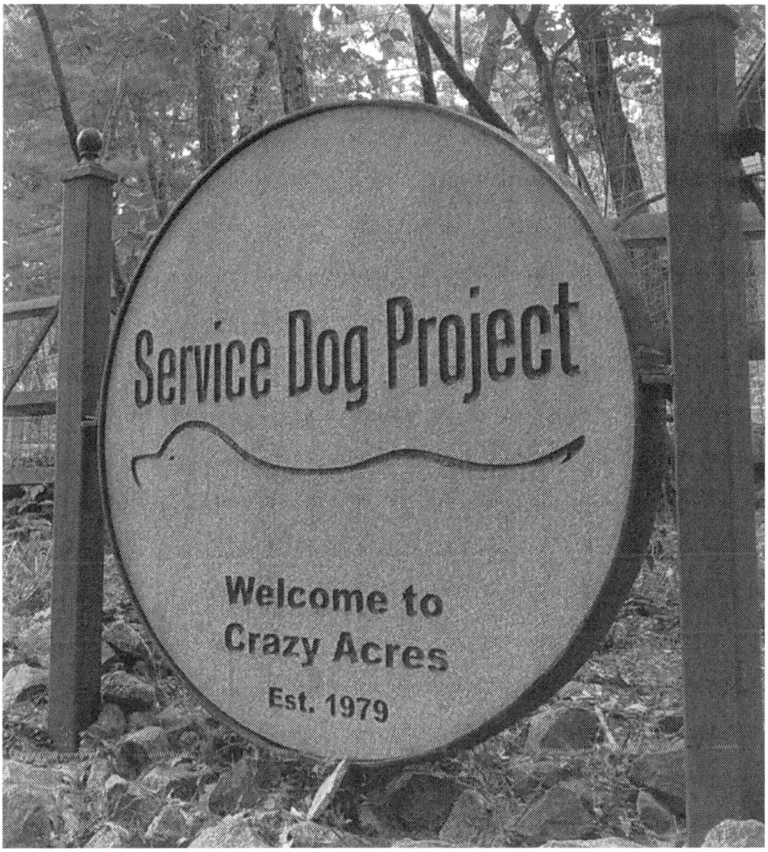
Service Dog Project
Welcome to
Crazy Acres
Est. 1979

Printed in Great Britain
by Amazon